The Carefree Life
自在的人生

Dharma Words
by
Venerable Master Hsing Yun

星雲大師法語

星雲大師 著

Translated by
Fo Guang Shan International Translation Center
佛光山國際翻譯中心翻譯

3456 South Glenmark Drive
Hacienda Heights, CA 91745
U.S.A.
Tel: 626-923-5143 Fax: 626-923-5145
Email: itc@blia.org

First edition, 1998; Revised edition, 2001.

Published by Hsi Lai University Press
3456 South Glenmark Drive
Hacienda Heights, CA 91745.
Telephone: 626-961-9697
Fax: 626-369-1944
Website: www.hlu.edu

Chinese by Venerable Master Hsing Yun
Translated into English from the Chinese by
Fo Guang Shan International Translation Center.
Cover design by Mei-chi Shih.

Revised edition
ISBN: 1-929192-04-5
Library of Congress Control Number: 2001087284

Printed in Los Angeles, California, U.S.A.

目 錄
Contents

Acknowledgements

We received a lot of help from many people and we want to thank all of them again here. We especially appreciate Venerable Tzu Jung, the Chief Executive of Fo Guang Shan International Translation Center, for her support and encouragement; Helen Tsai, Jeanne Tsai, and Amy Lam, for their translation; Susan Tidwell, Gordon Gibb, Madelon Wheeler-Gibb, Louvenia Ortega, and Ching Tay, for their proofreading. Last but not least, our gratitude also goes to Mei-chi Shih for her creative cover design. The help of these people was invaluable in making this publication possible and is very much appreciated.

自在的人生

在這個世界上，每個人每天同樣擁有二十四小時，有的人活得很愜意，有的過得很苦惱。為什麼同樣的日子，會產生快樂與煩惱的不同感受呢？主要在於各人面對生活的態度不同。所以，如何面對生活，就成為一個重要的課題。我有四項建議給各位參考：

第一，對感情要不執不捨：

經常有人問：「人怎麼會來到世間上的呢？」人是從情愛而來的！佛教講人叫做「有情眾生」，人既是有感情的動物，所以每個人皆離不開感情生活。縱然如此，我們對感情也應該要能做到不執不捨，也就是中庸之道，既不過於執著，為情所困，也不要捨棄感情，最好把感情昇華為對眾生的慈悲，這才是最美好的人性。

A Carefree Life

We all are allotted twenty-four hours each and every day. For some of us these are happy hours, while others find them quite bitter. Why do different people experience different feelings? The reason lies mainly in the diversity of attitudes we have toward life. Consequently, how we deal with life becomes an important issue. Here are four suggestions for you to consider:

1. Neither be attached to nor removed from affection

People often wonder by what means we come into this world. The answer is that we arrive as a result of emotion, especially love. In Buddhism, human beings are often referred to as sentient beings, and as such are creatures of affection. Therefore, no one leads a life devoid of feelings. Nevertheless, we must strive to be neither attached nor indifferent when handling our feelings. This is the middle path. We should not be trapped by affection nor should we disregard emotion. The best path is to transform our affection for a few into kindness and com-

第二，對五欲要不拒不貪：

　　五欲：財、色、名、食、睡，乃是人類五種基本的欲望。對於這五種欲望，我們既無法完全捨棄，卻也不能過份的沉溺、縱欲，最好抱持既不排拒，也不貪求的態度，就像維摩居士「雖處居家，不著三界，示有妻子？常修梵行」，這才是我們對五欲應有的態度。．

第三，對世間要不厭不求：

　　在這個世間上，難免有順境有逆境，不管是苦是樂，我們應該要隨遇而安、隨緣生活，千萬不要有消極厭世的逃避心理，也不要有希求「長生不老」的妄想。

passion for all living beings.

2. Neither cast away nor cling to the five desires

Wealth, beauty, fame, food, and sleep are the five basic kinds of human desires. We cannot discard them completely nor should we indulge in them. The best way is neither to cast them away nor to crave them. The layman Vimala-kirti set a good example for us. He led a householder's life without clinging to the three realms of desire, form, and formlessness; he was married, yet always carried on his Buddhist practice. The middle path is the proper way of dealing with the five desires.

3. Neither detest nor make demands of the world

Life brings not only times of felicity but also times of mis-fortune. No matter how bitter or happy these times are, we should remain composed and live accord-ing to the circumstances. We should never adopt the escapist frame of mind of pessimism and abhorrence toward the world. Nor should we make unreasonable demands, such as wanting to live forever.

第四，對生死要不懼不迷：

有人說人生如戰場。在人生的旅途中，的確有許多的關卡要過，所謂名關、利關、生死關，關關難過。有的人在面對生死時，心生畏懼、迷惑，那是因為不能體悟生命的真諦。假如懂得生死一如的道理，便不再對生死感到畏懼、迷惑，一切就能自由自在了。

4. Neither be afraid of nor deluded by life and death

Someone once said that human life is like a battlefield, and in the journey of life, there are many barriers through which we must pass. There are the barriers of fame, fortune, life, and death. Every obstacle is difficult to overcome. When faced with the greatest of all hurdles — death, some people become frightened and confused. They do not understand the truth of existence: that life and death are, in reality, not different from each other. When we understand the meaning of life and death, we no longer need to be afraid or deluded. It is at this point that our lives can truly be carefree.

如何求得自在人生？就是：

第一，對感情要不執不捨。

第二，對五欲要不拒不貪。

第三，對世間要不厭不求。

第四，對生死要不懼不迷。

How can we lead a carefree life?

1. Neither be attached to nor removed from affection.
2. Neither cast away nor cling to the five desires.
3. Neither detest nor make demands of the world.
4. Neither be afraid of nor deluded by life and death.

般若的人生

現實的人生，每天早出晚歸，汲汲營營，為了追求功名富貴而辛勤忙碌，但到頭來卻又不知為何辛苦為何忙？如果有了「般若」，人生就不一樣了，所謂「平常一樣窗前月，纔有梅花便不同」。窗前的明月好美呀！再加上幾朵梅花掩映，境界就更不同了。生活中的穿衣、吃飯，如果有了般若，穿衣吃飯的味道也會不一樣。如何過般若的人生呢？

How to Apply Wisdom to Daily Life

In modern society, many of us live hurried lives, leaving home early in the morning and returning late at night, mainly in pursuit of fame and wealth. Yet, do we have the wisdom to know why we toil and labor? When we have wisdom, we are able to see life in an entirely different light. A Chinese saying reminds us, "The moon outside the window tonight is the same as on other nights; it is the plum blossoms that give it a different look." Although the moon outside the window is always wonderfully beautiful, it is even more striking when the flowers bloom. If we use wisdom when we are dressing and eating, we will have a completely different attitude about even these daily activities. How do we apply wisdom to our daily lives?

第一，用般若來處事：

　　我們做人處事，不光是用感情，也不光是用物質，而要用「般若」，「般若」就是智慧。比方說你有技能，你把技術傳授給別人；你有哲學的思想、有好的道理語句貢獻給別人，這就是般若。能用「般若」處事，做什麼事情都是好事、都是善事，不會有副作用。

1. Use wisdom to handle everyday situations

When we are dealing with others and handling our affairs, we cannot rely solely on our emotions nor can we operate on a purely material basis. We need to use wisdom. For example, if you have a special skill, you can teach others; if you have a good philosophy, you can attempt to share it with others. If we use wisdom accordingly, the results will always benefit others.

第二，用般若來思想：

　　一個人在舉心動念間，千萬不要存有貪欲、瞋恨、自私；不要處心積慮的算計別人，凡事能為別人著想，能用般若來思想，必能獲得別人的信賴、敬重。

2. Use wisdom to think

Whenever our thoughts arise, we need to be careful and never let greed, hatred, or selfishness remain in our minds. With all matters in life, we should be forthright, not deceptive or calculating. We should always think about others and apply wisdom to our ideas. This is how we earn the respect and trust of others.

第三，用般若來生活：

　　我們的生活裡如果有般若，吃飯的時候就能體會，「一粥一飯來處不易」，那麼這碗飯就會吃得很香，就覺得菜根有菜根的香味，就容易知足；相反

3. Use wisdom in our daily lives

We should apply wisdom to our daily lives. When we eat our meals with wisdom, we can then appreciate the hard work of many people who made it possible for us to consume the bowl of rice

的，如果你用不滿的心情來吃的話，即使珍饈美味也不覺得好吃。所以有了「般若」，忙，有忙的意義；奉獻，有奉獻的價值；同樣是穿衣吃飯，可是意義就不一樣了。

第四，用般若來教化：

目前佛光山的佛學院，有很多的青年學生報考，他們為什麼要讀佛教學院呢？就是想用般若的思想，想以智慧來教化人間，同時也充實自己的人生。

所以，般若的人生應該要：

第一，用般若來處事。

第二，用般若來思想。

第三，用般若來生活。

第四，用般若來教化。

before us. With such appreciation, we are certain to enjoy our food and feel a sense of contentment. On the other hand, if we are never satisfied, even a gourmet meal won't make us happy. With wisdom, our efforts will have a special meaning and our offerings will have special value. When we use wisdom, we look at the simplest activities, like dressing and eating, in a completely different light.

4. Use wisdom to educate

Currently, we have many applicants who wish to apply to the Buddhist College at Fo Guang Shan. Why do they want to enroll in the Buddhist College? They want to improve themselves. They want to learn about the philosophy of wisdom and how to use wisdom to educate others.

To live wisely, we should do the following:

1. Use wisdom to handle everyday situations.

2. Use wisdom to think.

3. Use wisdom in our daily lives.

4. Use wisdom to educate.

快樂的人生

大家都有一個共同的心理，即希望生活快樂。快樂是人人一致的希望，但是實際上並不是人人都能享有幸福快樂的人生。我們如何才會快樂？我提供以下四點意見：

第一，以捨為有：

有的人整天妄想、貪求，這樣的人生不會快樂；相反的，懂得喜捨的人生，快樂無窮。「捨」並不是完全給人，而是一種結緣，例如：我專心聽你講話，就是與你結緣；幫你做一件事情，給你一些助力，給你一個微笑，給你一個注目禮，都是結緣。

A Happy Life

We all have one desire in common — to lead a happy life. Everyone hopes to attain happiness, but in actuality, not everyone is able to live a life of happiness. How can we be happy? I would like to offer the following four principles:

1. Giving is receiving

Some people spend all their time dreaming about and chasing after things for themselves. A life spent on such greedy pursuits does not lead to happiness. It is by knowing how to give that we will be able to bring happiness into our lives. Giving does not mean that we must forgo everything we possess; giving also means forming good relationships with others. For example, I can listen attentively to you when you talk, help you to do a simple task, give you support, give you a smile, and regard you with respect. Offering these gestures establishes good relations between us.

所以，表面上看起來你是在給
人，其實是在播種福田。能夠
捨的人表示自己很富有，因為
你內心有感恩、有滿足，你才
肯捨，才肯給人。心中有好
話，才能說好話；心中有微
笑，臉上才有笑容，所以「以
捨為有」，才會快樂。

Although it may seem as though you are only giving, receiving nothing in return, in reality you are cultivating your own field of merits. If you can give to others, you are really quite rich. How can this be so? It is because you willingly offer the gift of consideration and are thankful and content. Your heart is filled with goodness, so you use only positive words. Your heart is also filled with delight, so your face radiates with the bright light of joy. Through the pleasure you feel and the merits you receive from giving, you can experience great joy.

第二，以忙為樂：

一般人喜歡偷閒，其實偷閒是
苦，忙才會快樂。有人常問
我：這麼多年不見了，您怎麼
一點也沒有老呢？我回答：我
很忙，沒有時間老啊！因為忙
得很快樂，忙得樂以忘憂，所
以不知老之將至。

2. Being engaged is happiness

Typically, people think they enjoy being idle when, in fact, idleness fosters suffering. It is only by being fully engaged that one is able to experience happiness. People often make the following remark to me: "We haven't seen each other for so many years, but you haven't aged one bit. How do you do it?" I reply, "I am very busy. I have no time to get old." Staying engaged gives me great happiness and makes me forget my worries, and because of this, I do not realize that I am growing older.

第三，以勤為富：

一般人都希望自己發財，其實只要肯勤勞，就是一種財富；不勤勞，即使擁有萬貫家財，也會坐吃山空，所以要「以勤為富」。

第四，以忍為力：

佛祖之所以是佛祖，因為他「難忍能忍，難行能行」。所謂「三祇修福慧，百劫修相好」，一個人能夠忍，就有力量。所以我們要能忍苦、忍難、忍饑、忍餓、忍早、忍晚，要「以忍為力」，一忍萬事成。

3. Hard work is wealth

Most people wish to possess great riches, but they often do not realize that a willingness to work hard is a kind of wealth. Even if you possess a great fortune, unless you continue to work hard, you risk losing everything.

4. Perseverance is strength

How did the Buddha achieve supreme enlightenment? He was able to endure the bitterest of ordeals and perform the most difficult tasks. In their path to Buddhahood, even Bodhisattvas must cultivate virtue and wisdom over countless eons and another hundred kalpas before they can eventually be adorned with the thirty-two signs of perfection. When one can persevere, one is truly powerful. Therefore, to be successful in every aspect of our lives, we must learn to bear suffering, hardship, hunger, and hard work. Having the strength of perseverance helps us to endure happily.

快樂的人生是可以由自己創造的，只要我們懂得：

第一，以捨為有。

第二，以忙為樂。

第三，以勤為富。

第四，以忍為力。

We can create happy lives for ourselves as long as we practice the following four principles:

1. Giving is receiving.

2. Being engaged is happiness.

3. Hard work is wealth.

4. Perseverance is strength.

快樂之道

追求快樂,是一般人生活中最重要的目標。一個人如果擁有財富、健康,乃至兒女成群、子孫滿堂,卻獨缺快樂,生命將失去意義。所以擁有快樂,可以說是人生最美好的事情。如何擁有快樂?

第一,不要把煩惱帶到床上:

任何人都有煩惱,但是千萬不要把煩惱帶到床上,因為這樣只有徒使自己輾轉反側,徹夜難眠,並不能解決煩惱。白天縱有不滿意的人事困擾,到了睡覺的時候,至少要把它放下,不要帶到床上。

上了床,就要好好地、安安靜靜地睡覺,睡眠充足,身體健康,快樂就會隨之而來。

第二,不要把怨恨留到明天:

人和人之間,總會有一些芥蒂、不滿意。但不要把今天的仇恨留到明天,甚至牢記在心,耿耿於懷。佛經上說出家

The Path to Happiness

Attaining of happiness is the most important goal for most of us. Suppose we had wealth, good health, children, grandchildren, and the like, but we did not have happiness: our life would lack meaning. Therefore, to have happiness is the most wonderful thing in life. How can we attain happiness?

1. Do not take worries to bed

Although everyone has problems, unhappy thoughts should never be taken to bed. Doing so only results in sleeplessness and does little to resolve the problems. At bedtime, one should not think about the difficulties experienced during the day, instead, one should focus on getting a good night's sleep. We are always healthier and happier after a good night's rest.

2. Do not carry over thoughts of hatred from one day to the next

Sometimes ill feelings are created during social interaction. It is important that we do not cling to the grudges of yesterday, or even the ones of many years

人「無隔宿之仇」，也就是說不要留滯任何仇恨在心中。一個人如果心中充滿仇恨，不但交不到好朋友，也感受不到人生的樂趣。

第三，不要把愛心縱容邪惡：

邪惡是不正當的，如果你用愛心去包容邪惡，那就鑄成大錯了。

第四，不要把慈悲施予非法：

我們對人要慈悲，指的是對正當的人、正當的事情要慈悲。至於對非法的人、非法的事則不能縱容，不能施予慈悲，否則就失去了慈悲的意義。慈悲要有智慧，要能分辨是非、好壞，才是真慈悲。

past. The sutras teach that monastics should not carry resentment from one day over to the next. This means that we must avoid keeping any anger or hatred in our minds. A person who is full of hatred will be bereft of good friends and unable to feel joy in life.

3. Do not suffer evil out of love

Evil is always wrong and improper. To endure evil out of love is to err grossly. This will never lead to happiness.

4. Do not tolerate lawlessness out of kindness and compassion

We must be kind and compassionate toward one another. However, we must take care to give of ourselves only to righteous people and for wholesome matters. The meaning of kindness and compassion is lost when we tolerate lawlessness in their name. True kindness and compassion are always based on wisdom. To be able to judge right from wrong and good from bad will bring us happiness.

快樂之道有四點：

第一，不要把煩惱帶到床上。

第二，不要把怨恨留到明天。

第三，不要把愛心縱容邪惡。

第四，不要把慈悲施予非法。

Thus, the path to happiness has four components:

1. Do not take worries to bed.
2. Do not carry over thoughts of hatred from one day to the next.
3. Do not suffer evil out of love.
4. Do not tolerate lawlessness out of kindness and compassion.

休息旅行的利益

The Benefits of Leisure Travel

在緊張忙碌的生活中，偶而有休息的時間，有旅行的時間，對我們生命的再出發、再精進是頗有用處的。我們出外旅行、參訪，有何利益呢?

In the midst of our tense and busy lives, occasionally taking time for leisure travel can rejuvenate us, so that we may resume our journey in life with renewed vigor. What benefits do we receive by taking time to experience new places and meet new people to us?

第一，讀萬卷書，行萬里路：

俗話說：「讀萬卷書，行萬里路」，出外旅行，不論是接觸大自然，還是拓展人際關係，都能增進我們的知識。

1. We experience nature and enrich ourselves

Folklore says: "Reading thousands of volumes of books cannot compare to traveling thousands of miles of road." Traveling allows us to experience the immensity of nature and to expand our interpersonal relationships. These experiences will increase our knowledge and deepen our understanding of the world.

第二，擴大心胸，放寬視野：

當我們旅行、參訪時，要能用開闊的心胸、心量去接受外界的景觀、風俗習慣，擴大自己的視野，而且要能看得廣、看得寬，包含歷史的背景、地理的常識與社會的風俗人情。

2. We broaden our minds and expand our awareness of others

While traveling and visiting others, we must maintain an unbiased mind so that we can impartially observe the scenery and be open to learning about the customs and traditions of others. This will allow us to expand our own capability to perceive and understand people and situations in a broader and deeper sense, including the historical background, geography, and social customs of the places we visit.

第三，能動能靜，能近能遠：

我們在旅行參學時，有時候要能靜，很靜態的去欣賞;有時候要能動，像爬山、涉水時，不計千里迢迢。所謂能近能遠，是近處的我們要用心去研究，遠處的也不放過機會去瞭解。

3. We are able to be active or quiet, close or distant

When we travel, there are times to maintain quietude so that we can appreciate our surroundings in tranquility. There are other times when dynamic action is appropriate. We may want to hike a great distance, follow a long and winding river, or climb to soaring heights. To be close and to be distant means that we attend to things nearby with utmost care, yet, at the same time, we never miss an opportunity to deepen our understanding of things far away. Leisure travel will help us to develop this flexibility of awareness.

第四，溪聲山色，任性遨遊：

「溪聲盡是廣長舌，山色無非清淨身」，大自然給了我們許多的心得。比方說：一個參禪者，沒有參禪的時候，看山是

4. We more fully enjoy the sounds of brooks and the colors of mountains

"The sounds made by brooks all expound the Dharma; the colors of the mountains are mani-

山，看水是水；參禪後，看山不是山，看水不是水；要一直等到悟道之後，他才能看山又是山，看水又是水了。

人生的經驗智慧，常在休息旅行中也能得到。

適度的休息旅行，所具有的利益是：

第一，讀萬卷書，行萬里路。

第二，擴大心胸，放寬視野。

第三，能動能靜，能近能遠。

第四，溪聲山色，任性遨遊。

festations of the pure body of ultimate reality." Great nature offers us profound inspiration, as the following experience of a Ch'an student illustrates: Before traveling to seek instruction, one sees a mountain as a mountain and water as water. After seeking Ch'an instruction, the student does not see a mountain as a mountain or water as water. Finally, only after awakening to the truth, will he or she once again see a mountain as a mountain and water as water. When we venture out and see more of the world, it is easier for us to experience this type of awareness.

Therefore, the wisdom of experience is often obtained through leisure travel.

Appropriate rest and travel facilitates our development in the following ways:

1. We experience nature and enrich ourselves.
2. We broaden our minds and expand our awareness of others.
3. We are able to be active or quiet, close or distant.
4. We more fully enjoy the sounds of brooks and the colors of mountains.

覺悟的生活

我們每天都要生活，有的人糊裡糊塗的過一生，有的人卻潛心於研究自己為什麼要活著？這就是追求覺悟的生活。覺悟的生活對我們是非常重要的，如何過一個覺悟的生活呢？我提供四點意見：

第一，要自己承擔：

所謂覺悟的生活，是自己要承擔生活的責任，不要將責任推卸給別人；不是把有利的事情都歸於自己，把對自己不利的事情都推給別人。例如有人開會遲到了，就會拿一大堆理由來搪塞，像交通擁塞、下傾盆大雨、朋友來訪或忽然有電話…等，他不肯承擔遲到的責任，卻全部歸咎於別人或其他事情上。所以我覺得，生活的意義在於自己承擔。

An Enlightened Life

As our lives pass from day to day, some of us drift aimlessly while others strive diligently to discover the meaning of their existence. The latter is pursued by one who lives an enlightened life. It is a very important way of living. How do we lead such a life? I suggest the following four guidelines:

1. Shoulder responsibilities

To lead an enlightened life, we must shoulder responsibilities instead of passing them on to others. Furthermore, we must not keep only the favorable for ourselves and push the unfavorable on to others. For example, a person late for a meeting may give many excuses for tardiness, such as traffic congestion, heavy rain, a visit from a friend, or an unexpected phone call. Unwilling to assume the responsibility of being tardy, this person blames others. That is why I say the meaning of life is realized through assuming responsibilities.

第二，要隨緣放曠：

在生活中，不要太執著，不要把自己繃得太緊，不要劃地自限；有時候，一個人要想到整個家庭，也要想到社會，甚至進一步想到國家及芸芸眾生。如果能夠常常心懷國家、眾生，你的心胸自然就能寬大起來，心胸寬大，自然能隨緣放曠。

第三，要明白自己：

人最可憐的就是不明白自己。有時我們常責怪他人，怪他人不瞭解我們，其實我們自己又何嘗瞭解自己、認識自己、明白自己呢？所以我們要能將自己整理得有條不紊，看得清清楚楚：我的慈悲有多少？我的智慧有多少？我的力量有多少？能夠明白自己，也就離覺悟不遠了。

2. Live according to circumstances and keep an open mind

In our daily lives, we should not be stubborn or rigid; nor should we restrict our concerns only to ourselves. There are times when a person must also consider the family, the community, and, even further, the nation and all sentient beings. When we constantly care about the well-being of others, we broaden our perspective. Subsequently, we are able to live in harmony with our circumstances.

3. Understand ourselves

The most lamentable human defect is our failure to understand ourselves. We sometimes accuse others of not understanding us when, in fact, we often neither understand nor know ourselves very deeply. If we control ourselves and behave in an orderly manner, we will understand ourselves more clearly. To do this, we must ask ourselves some difficult questions. How kind and compassionate am I? How much wisdom and strength do I really have? If we understand ourselves, we are not far from awakening.

第四，要珍惜生活：

　所謂珍惜生活就是珍惜自己。珍惜生活，是因為我們的生活很寶貴。在生活裡，不浪費時間就是珍惜生活，物盡其用就是珍惜生活，不蹧蹋人情就是珍惜生活。

所以，覺悟的生活就是：

第一，要自己承擔。

第二，要隨緣放曠。

第三，要明白自己。

第四，要珍惜生活。

4. Treasure life

　Life is indeed very precious, and treasuring life is cherishing oneself. How do we treasure life? To conserve time is to treasure life; to conserve resources is to treasure life; to conserve friendship is to treasure life.

Therefore, when we have an enlightened life, we do the following:

1. Shoulder responsibilities
2. Live according to circumstances and keep an open mind.
3. Understand ourselves.
4. Treasure life.

美滿家庭

怎樣建設美滿的家庭？家庭最重要的是和諧、美滿，人我之間相處得非常親愛，所以美滿家庭的條件有四項：

第一，以慈悲獲得尊重：

家庭裡的每一個成員要想獲得別人的尊重，自己必須先以慈悲心尊重他人，就是現在我們所講的愛。家庭裡，最重要的是每一份子都要有愛，甚至於養的貓、狗，如果你對牠有愛心的話，牠的發育、成長都會不一樣，花草也如同貓、狗，只要你細心澆水，照顧它，則能百花盛開，果實飽滿，所以慈悲才能獲得尊重。

A Happy Family

Harmony, happiness, contentment, and affection among family members are all very important components of a happy family. On what then is a happy family built? The foundation of a happy family includes the following four essential elements:

1. Earn respect through kindness and compassion

To gain respect from other family members, we must first treat them with kindness and compassion. This is what we call love. Every family member needs love. Even the growth and development of a dog or cat will improve if you attend to the animal with loving care. Plants are no different. If you water and take good care of them, they will bloom to their fullest and bear plump fruit. Thus, by being compassionate and kind to others, they will thrive and, in turn, repay us with their respect and love.

第二，以智慧處理是非：

家庭中有很多的成員，男女老少各有不同的性格、不同的觀念，所以是非不斷，那麼如何來處理是非呢?就是用智慧。比方說我們不要聽是非，不說是非，不傳是非，當然我們就不怕是非。所謂「是非朝朝有，不聽自然無」，是非止於智者，因此一個家庭如果沒有是非，大家必定能和平相處。

第三，以恭敬接待大眾：

家庭中人來客去，即使是家人的朋友也應該表示一種適當的恭敬。你恭敬別人，同樣地，家裡的份子也會恭敬你，所以佛法常常講「佛法在恭敬中求」。《法華經》裡，有位常不輕菩薩，見到人就合掌、禮拜說：「我不敢輕視汝等，汝等皆當做佛。」我們對家人人格的尊重，就是美滿家庭的重要條件。

2. Handle conflict with wisdom

Every family member, whether male, female, elderly, or young, has his or her own unique personality and point of view. As a result, disagreements arise. How should one deal with these disagreements? Simply put, with wisdom. If we do not listen to, speak of, or engage in trifling disputes, then we do not need to worry about conflicts. As the saying goes, "Trifling disputes, day after day; ignore them, they will go away." This is why we say disputes stop with the wise. When a family is free of disputes, everyone lives in peace.

3. Treat everyone with respect

When friends of the family visit, they should be treated with respect. When you respect others, they will respect you. It is often said in Buddhism that "the Buddhist teachings are realized through respect." In the Lotus Sutra, the Never Disparaging Bodhisattva pays reverence to everyone he sees, saying "I dare not look down on you as you will become a Buddha." Showing respect for each family member's individuality is an important element of a happy family.

第四，以道德修養身心：

我們要有德，要有道，身心才會安定、安穩，形成美滿家庭。

因此美滿家庭四要件是：

第一，以慈悲獲得尊重。

第二，以智慧處理是非。

第三，以恭敬接待大眾。

第四，以道德修養身心。

4. Cultivate body and mind with morality

Guided by morals and principles, our body and mind can become settled, stable, and steady. This is the foundation of a happy family.

The four essential ingredients of a happy family are as follows:

1. Earn respect through kindness and compassion.
2. Handle conflict with wisdom.
3. Treat everyone with respect.
4. Cultivate body and mind with morality.

看心

我們平常看山，看水，看
花，看草，看人，看事，看盡
男男女女，看盡人間萬象，卻
很少人「看心」。因為儘管我
們看盡了世界上的美景奇觀，
卻看不到自己的「心」！心是
我們自己的，我們要能明心見
性，才能找到自己。

六祖大師在《法寶壇經》裡，
有四句話，教我們看心：

第一，聖人求心不求佛：

聖人看心，不一定要求佛；他
向自己要求，不向佛求。有一
首詩偈說：「佛在靈山莫遠
求，靈山就在汝心頭；人人有
個靈山塔，好向靈山塔下修。」
求自己，比求佛重要，開發自

Look at the Mind

Ordinarily, we look at mountains, water, flowers, grass, and
other people. We see all sorts of
things: all kinds of men and
women and all varieties of world-
ly phenomena. However, very few
of us actually "look at the mind."
Even if we have seen all the
wonderful, beautiful scenery of
the world, we probably have yet
to see our own internal landscape
and look at our own minds! After
all, our minds are ourselves.
Therefore, to understand our own
mind and to reveal our Buddha
nature is to discover ourselves.

The Sixth Patriarch of the Ch'an
school taught the following four
points in the *Platform Sutra* on
how to look at the mind:

1. Sages look to the mind rather than plead to the Buddha for help

When a sage looks at his own
mind, he is not looking externally
to the Buddha for help. He asks of
himself rather than of the Buddha.
A gatha says: "Do not look for the

己佛性的潛能，比終日空想成佛卻不去修行實踐更要緊。

Buddha on faraway Vulture Peak: Vulture Peak is right in your mind. Each of us has Vulture Peak within; we should look toward our own Vulture peak to practice our cultivation." Relying on ourselves is more important than pleading with the Buddha. Realizing our own Buddha nature through practice is far more important than simply daydreaming about becoming a Buddha.

第二，愚人求佛不求心：

愚痴的人天天求佛拜神，跟神明求平安、求發財、求順利，這是把信仰建築在貪心上面。一個人如果不反求諸己，不觀照自己的內心，不淨化自己的心，求佛有什麼用？

2. Fools plead with the Buddha rather than look to the mind

Foolish people plead with the Buddha and worship deities day after day, asking for peace, security, material wealth, and for an easy time in life. These people's beliefs are founded on greed. If we do not deeply reflect upon ourselves and purify our own minds, what is the use of pleading to the Buddha?

第三，智人調心不調身：

有智慧的人，平常就懂得治心，因為心為一切萬法之本，所以平時要以戒來對治貪心；以定來對治瞋心；以慧來對治癡心，這樣妄心就調伏了。心一調治好，相貌自然端莊。

3. Sages regulate the mind rather than the body

Wise people discipline their minds, because they know that the mind is the origin of all phenomena. Therefore, at all times, we must control the mind of greed with precepts, control the mind of anger with meditative concentration, and control the mind of ignorance with wisdom. Then, our delusive mind will be under control. Once our mind is harmonious, our physical appearance naturally becomes dignified.

第四，愚人調身不調心：

愚痴的人往往只注重身體的保健，只知道要注意營養、運動等保健之道。調身雖然要緊，調心更重要。如果只調身不調心，心沒有治好，光有健康的身體而沒有好心，這個身體不會做好事。如果把心治好，就算身體不健康，但有清淨的思惟，有善良的言行，他的生活自然就能解脫。

4. Fools regulate the body rather than the mind

Foolish people pay attention only to physical health. They focus only on how to improve their body through nutrition and exercise. Although taking care of our physical health is important, regulating the mind is even more important. If we only take care of our bodies without nourishing our minds, our minds will suffer. A healthy body without a good mind will do us very little good. However, if we nurture our minds well, even when our bodies are not healthy, we can still have pure thinking, wholesome speech, and virtuous actions, and we will still be able to liberate ourselves.

所以，看心的四種方法就是：

第一，聖人求心不求佛。

第二，愚人求佛不求心。

第三，智人調心不調身。

第四，愚人調身不調心。

Therefore, the four ways of seeing the mind are as follows:

1. Sages look to the mind, rather than plead to the Buddha for help.
2. Fools plead with the Buddha rather than look to the mind.
3. Sages regulate the mind rather than the body.
4. Fools regulate the body rather than the mind.

淨化心靈

今天的社會到處充滿污染，處在染濁、複雜的環境裡，我們如何淨化自己的心靈呢？有四個方法：

第一，用捨心對治貪欲：

我們的貪心、自私心，都是因為執著「我」而起。我要名、要利，要所有一切對我有利的事與物，處處都是為自己著想，因此變得貪婪自私。假如我們現在能換成一種捨心：把我的利益和你分享，把我的知識傳授給你，有了捨心，貪欲心自然越來越少，心地自然清明，所以要以捨心來對治貪欲。

第二，用慈心對治暴力：

今天的社會，到處充斥暴力，你看他一眼，他就給你一拳；你不小心碰他一下，他就戳你一刀，到處充滿暴戾之氣。如

Purifying the Mind

Our modern society is replete with polluting influences: greed, violence, false views, and chaos. While existing in such a turbid, debased, and complicated environment, how can we purify our own minds? There are four ways:

1. Counter greed with a mind of renunciation

Our greed and selfishness arise from our attachment to "self." We often think, "I want fame, profit, and all things and matters beneficial to me." When we think only of ourselves in every situation, we are being greedy and selfish. If we can assume a mind of renunciation, share our profits, and pass on our knowledge to others, then our greed will diminish and, naturally our minds will become pure. Therefore, we must counter greed with a mind of renunciation.

2. Counter violence with a mind of compassion

In today's society we are surrounded by violence. If you stare at someone, you are likely to have a fist shaken at you; if you acci-

何消除暴力？我們不能以暴制暴，應該學習諸佛菩薩以慈眼視眾生，你有慈悲心，自然可以儡服暴力。所以今天的社會，希望有更多的人有慈悲心，以此來對治暴力。

dentally touch someone, you are at risk of being stabbed. How can we extinguish this violence? It cannot be countered by using more violence. We must learn to do what all Buddhas and Bodhisattvas do see all sentient beings through compassionate eyes. As long as we have compassion in our hearts, we can successfully subdue violence. Therefore, we hope more people in today's society can counter violence with minds of compassion

第三，用正心對治邪見：

今天的社會，到處充滿了邪見。知識有邪的知識，思想有邪的思想，甚至於信仰多是邪的信仰，由於邪知邪見，造成整個社會的紊亂、脫序。要對治邪見，必須要用正心，所謂「佛說一切法，為治一切心：若無一切心，何用一切法？」所以要有正心才能對治邪見。

3. Counter false views with the correct mindset

False views abound in modern society. These views include false knowledge, false thoughts, and false beliefs. Because of these false views, society is in a state of confusion and chaos. To counter falsehood, we must have the right mindset: an orientation based on the teachings. The following saying reminds us, "To treat our minds is the purpose of the Buddha's teachings; if we already had the right mindset, for what would the teachings be delivered?" Therefore, we need to use the right mindset to counter false views.

第四，用佛心對治混亂：

世界日益混亂，處在混亂的環境中，我們如何不迷亂？有了佛心，以佛心看世間，人人都是佛，世間就是佛土。

所以，淨化自己心靈的方法是：

第一，用捨心對治貪欲。

第二，用慈心對治暴力。

第三，用正心對治邪見。

第四，用佛心對治混亂。

4. Counter chaos with Buddha-mind

The world is becoming more chaotic day by day. While living in such a chaotic environment, how do we avoid being lost? By learning from the Buddha and viewing the world through our Buddha-mind, we then can appreciate that everyone is a Buddha and that the world is indeed the Buddha land. With this outlook, one can never be lost.

Therefore, the ways to purify one's mind are as follows:

1. Counter greed with a mind of renunciation.
2. Counter violence with a mind of compassion.
3. Counter false views with the correct mindset.
4. Counter chaos with Buddha-mind.

美化人心

現在社會大眾都很注重美化。如環境要美化、家庭要美化、人生要美化、語言要美化等等，其實我們的心更要美化。

如何美化人心呢？

第一，用平等的觀念來美化人心：

所謂平等，就是我不比你大、不比你多、不比你有、不比你好，我和你是一樣的。有了平等的觀念，我們就能尊重別人，幫助別人，就能守法，就能與人分工合作。

第二，用慚愧的觀念來美化人心：

慚愧羞恥之心，人皆有之。佛經說：「慚恥之服，無上莊嚴」。我們有了慚愧之心，就能恥自己有所不如、有所不能、有所不清淨、有所不善美。因為有了這份慚愧心，所

Beautifying Our Minds

In today's society, beautification is highly valued. We beautify our environment, our homes, our lives, our language, and so on. In actuality, we also need to beautify our minds.

How can we beautify our minds?

1. Beautify our minds with equality

Equality means to realize that we are not more important, more knowledgeable, wealthier, or better than others. We are ultimately the same as others. Once we have the mindset that all people are equal, we can then respect others, help others, abide the law, and cooperate with others.

2. Beautify our minds with repentance

All human beings have the capacity to experience remorse and humility. Buddhist sutras state: "Donning the robe of remorse and humility is the ultimate beautification." With the mind of repentance, we are capable of regretting our lack of under-

以能知恥圖強，改過向善。

第三，用感恩的觀念來美化人心：

懂得感恩的人，表示自己富有。平時我們可以說好話，做好事，給人方便，給人歡喜來表示感恩。

第四，用慈悲的觀念來美化人心：

所謂慈悲，就是我保護你的生存，不讓你受到侵犯；我幫助老弱，使老弱婦孺都有所依靠；我救濟危難，扶持正義，仗義直言，主持公道，這些都能美化我們的心。

standing, capability, purity, and perfection. Repentance infuses us with the determination to strengthen ourselves by mending our wrongdoings and turning over a new leaf.

3. Beautify our minds with appreciation

People who know how to appreciate others show that they are truly rich within. We can express our appreciation by saying kind things, doing good deeds, providing others with convenience, and giving others joyfulness.

4. Beautify our minds with compassion

Compassion means to protect others and to prevent them from being harmed. It means that we help the elderly and the weak, making sure that they, along with other helpless adults and children, are well supported. We make sure that we save those in peril, support the virtuous, defend righteous causes, and maintain justice. All these compassionate acts can beautify our minds.

所以，美化人心之道有：

第一，用平等的觀念來美化人心。

第二，用慚愧的觀念來美化人心。

第三，用感恩的觀念來美化人心。

第四，用慈悲的觀念來美化人心。

Therefore, the ways to beautify our minds are as follows:

1. Beautify our minds with equality.
2. Beautify our minds with repentance.
3. Beautify our minds with appreciation.
4. Beautify our minds with compassion.

如何進步

進步是人人所希望的，包括事業上的進步、學業上的進步、道德上的進步、人格上的進步。人總想自己能步步高升，可是進步必須有進步的條件，什麼是進步的條件呢？

第一，要自省自責：

進步不能靠別人來給予，我們自己要自我不斷的反省、不斷的責備、不斷的要求，在自我不斷的自省、自責與要求之下，我們的道德、學問才會有進步。

第二，要自立自強：

進步不能光靠別人，也不能光靠上天來給予。進步是靠自己的辛苦、勤勞、奮鬥才能獲得，所以必須要自立，建立自我的信心、自我的觀念、思想與正見，然後自強。俗話說：

How to Make Progress

Everyone hopes to make progress toward their goals. We want to improve in various areas of life, such as careers, schoolwork, morals, and character. Progress, however, is based on certain conditions. What are the conditions that facilitate progress?

1. Progress requires self-reflection and self-evaluation

We cannot rely on others to make our progress for us. We must constantly examine, appraise, and require more of ourselves. Only by diligently practicing self-reflection and self-evaluation, and by continuously making demands on ourselves, can we progress in strengthening our morals and broadening our knowledge.

2. Progress requires self-support and self-striving

One cannot rely solely on others, nor can one rely just on heaven to provide progress. Progress can only be achieved by one's own labor, perseverance, and striving. Therefore, we must be independent, establishing per-

「天助人助，不如自助。」

sonal trust, personal ideas and thoughts, and correct views before we can become strong. A proverb says: "Heavenly help or help from others is no match for self-help."

第三，要自尊自信：

要求進步，但自己沒有自尊心、自信心，怎能進步呢？所以對自己要覺得我能，相信我能，有了自我的尊重、自我的信心才能有所成就。

3. Progress requires self-respect and self-confidence

Progress cannot be achieved without self-respect and self-confidence. Therefore, we each must convince ourselves that "I can" and then proceed to base all actions on this belief that "I can." Only through self-respect and self-confidence can achievement be accomplished.

第四，要自教自悟：

進步是要自己來教導自己，自己做自己的工程師、教師、美術師，來美化自己的語言、思想、威儀、智慧與知識，這樣才能有自我的覺悟。每個人每天都要有一點覺悟：「我懂了，我知道了！」不斷的覺悟，才會健全自己前進的步伐。

4. Progress requires self-teaching and self-awakening

Progress requires us to teach ourselves. We must be our own architect, teacher, and artist for beautifying our own language, thoughts, appearance, wisdom and knowledge. This is how we can attain self-awakening. Everybody should have a little awakening each day: "Oh! I understand, I know." With continuous awakening, we will be sure to maintain the pace of progress.

自我進步四法門是：

第一，要自省自責。

第二，要自立自強。

第三，要自尊自信。

第四，要自教自悟。

The four key requirements for self-progress are as follows:

1. Self-reflection and self-evaluation.
2. Self-support and self-striving.
3. Self-respect and self-confidence.
4. Self-teaching and self-awakening.

如何靠自己

How to Rely on Oneself

一般人都是心向外求，一心只希望別人幫我，只要求國家給我，要求社會大眾給我。一切靠別人、靠親友、靠社會、靠國家，自己內心沒有一點力量，一旦失去外在的支助就喪失前進的力量，這太脆弱了。所以人還是要靠自己，自己才是最可靠的朋友。

如何靠自己？健全自己？

Many people tend to seek help outside of themselves. Depending on others for assistance, they make demands on everyone: relatives, friends, and society. When a person relies completely on the support of others, he or she may become short on inner strength and may lose the ability to continue on with life once the external support is withdrawn. It is too precarious to always count on others. Therefore, we all must learn to depend on ourselves — the most reliable friend of all.

What skills do we need in order to rely on ourselves? In other words, how do we establish self-fulfillment?

第一，要自我肯定：

一個人如果連自己都不能肯定自己的道德、自己的學問、自己的能力、自己的發心、自己的慈悲，又怎能期望別人信任、肯定自己？

1. We must affirm ourselves

If we cannot even affirm our own moral values, knowledge, ability, motivation, and compassion, then how can we expect others to grant us their trust and approval?

第二，要自我尊重：

君子不重則不威，自重以後別人才會尊重我們。例如：說話

2. We must respect ourselves

When we do not respect ourselves, we lack dignity. A person

要說有份量的話，做事要做對人有益的事，才會贏得別人的尊重。

must first have self-respect before he or she can gain it from others. To earn the respect of others, our speech should be meaningful and our actions should be beneficial to others.

第三，要自我自在：

現在的人，常因別人一句話、一個臉色就坐立不安，困擾不已。佛教中有「一屁打過江」的故事，是說唐宋古文八大家之一的蘇東坡，自以為自己參禪的境界已經到達「八風吹不動」，沒想到卻被佛印禪師一屁就打過江，所以我們要自我自在，不要隨便受到影響。

3. We must be at ease with ourselves

Sometimes we become agitated because of a minor comment or a perceived slight from others. A well-known Buddhist story, "Blown Across the River by a Stir of Air," tells of such an incident involving Su Dongpo, one of the eight famous poets of the Tang and Sung dynasties: Su Dongpo thought he had mastered meditation to the point where he would no longer be influenced by others. Su never imagined that one subtle comment from Ch'an master Fo-yin would send him rushing across the river in anger! Likewise, we should all learn to be at ease with ourselves and not be easily irritated by others.

第四，要自我安樂：

現代人往往把快樂建立在外在的聲色娛樂上，或者仰賴別人的給予，自己內心全然沒有快

4. We must be happy and peaceful with ourselves

We frequently base our happiness on sensory amusements or on receiving things from others.

樂，所以，有時候會覺得活得沒有任何意義。如果我們能像佛教裡的許多禪師，雖然打坐時眼睛閉起來，不看不聽，但是內心卻很快樂。這種發自內心的法喜安樂，才是涵養生命的重要資糧。

Then, when these things are absent, we have very little sense of inner joy and may even believe that life is meaningless. However, if we can be like Ch'an masters who are full of inner joy even though they keep their eyes closed and refrain from seeing and hearing during meditation, then we, too, can find happiness and serenity. Such peace and Dharma joy generated from within is the ultimate way to nurture our lives.

所以，要健全自我，應該：

第一，要自我肯定。

第二，要自我尊重。

第三，要自我自在。

第四，要自我安樂。

Therefore, to rely on oneself, one must do the following:

1. We must affirm ourselves.
2. We must respect ourselves.
3. We must be at ease with ourselves.
4. We must be happy and peaceful with ourselves.

如何濟危扶弱

我們見到世人有危難，要去救濟他；見到幼小的弱者，要去扶助他。「惻隱之心，人皆有之」。所謂慈悲之念，人人都應該具足的。因此如何濟危扶弱呢？有四點意見：

第一，對生命要護其生存：

凡是有生命的東西，不要說一個人，就是一隻鳥、一條魚、一隻蜻蜓、一隻蝴蝶、一隻小麻雀，只要是有生命的東西，我們都要保護他的生存。現在講究環保生態，我們如果殘殺生命，就會影響全世界的生態平衡，害人也害己。

How to Save the Imperiled and Support the Weak

When we see people in danger or difficulty, we should save them. When we see small, young, weak ones, we should support them. As described in the saying, "All human beings have the heart of sympathy," the thought of compassion is already present in everyone. How then do we proceed to save the imperiled and support the weak? Here are four ways:

1. Protect all lives to ensure their survival

We should protect and ensure the survival of all lives, be it the life of a person, a bird, a fish, a dragonfly, a butterfly, or even a tiny sparrow. As we place great emphasis on environmental conservation and ecology today, we should be mindful that when we take a life, we are upsetting the ecological balance of the entire world. Ultimately, when we harm others, we harm ourselves.

第二，對老弱要拯其康強：

　　每一個人都會老，每一個生命都是很脆弱的，因此對老弱的生命，我們要幫助他，要使他健全，使他康強，所謂「老有所歸，幼有所養」。

第三，對危難要濟其平安：

　　有人游泳遭遇到滅頂的危險時，我要關心救生；有人開車太快，或是駕駛技術不好，我們提醒他嚴守交通規則；現在社會治安不好，我們要守望相助，要幫助隔壁鄰居，大家都能關心社區的安全。

第四，對邪見要助其正信：

　　很多人眼見社會動盪，生命無依，大家總想有個宗教信仰，但是信錯了對象，種種邪見，缺乏正信，是非常危險的。因此，我們對邪見的人要幫助他建立正信，就是相信實在的，

2. Help the elderly and the weak to be healthy and strong

Everyone grows old inevitably. Life is very fragile. Therefore, we should help the old and the weak to become healthy and strong. It has been said that "the elderly should be sheltered; the young should be nurtured."

3. Provide those in danger and difficulty with safety and security

When a swimmer is in peril of drowning, we should focus our efforts on saving that person. When someone drives too fast or recklessly, we need to remind him or her to obey the traffic rules. Security in society is an increasingly difficult matter. We must assist our neighbors; always watching out for and helping each other. The security of the community is everyone's concern.

4. Help those with evil views to establish correct beliefs

Many people who witness the instability of society and feel the insecurity of life seek solace in a religious belief. However, they may have misguided devotion by adopting evil views and lacking

相信有歷史的，相信有能力的。

correct beliefs. This is very dangerous. Therefore, we should help people who hold evil views to establish correct beliefs, to believe in what is real, to believe in the historical, and to believe in those capable of guiding others to better themselves.

所以，如何濟危扶弱？
就是：

第一，對生命要護其生存。

第二，對老弱要拯其康強。

第三，對危難要濟其平安。

第四，對邪見要助其正信。

Therefore, the four ways to save the imperiled and support the weak are as follows:

1. Protect all lives to ensure their survival.
2. Help the elderly and the weak to be healthy and strong.
3. Provide those in danger and difficulty with safety and security.
4. Help those with evil views to establish correct beliefs.

如何改變
自己的命運

我們常常看到有人去找相命師求卦算命，其實自己的命運，別人不一定算得準，自己的命運操縱在自己手裡，自己可以決定自己的命運。怎麼樣改變我們的命運呢？

第一，一塊金錢可以改變人的命運：

一塊錢，如果拿去買一本書來看，因此懂得待人處事的道理，懂得創業發財的方法，命運就此改變了；一塊錢，如果拿去賭錢，賭輸了，打打殺殺惹來牢獄之災，一生就完了。所以一塊錢可以決定人的命運。

How to Change Your Own Destiny

Some people go to fortune-tellers to have their futures divined or foretold. In reality, however, the destiny of a person cannot be accurately predicted by others. Our destinies are in our own hands. We each decide our own future. How then can you change your destiny?

1. A dollar can change your destiny

Suppose you used a dollar for buying a book, and after reading the book, you learned how to conduct yourself and handle money matters. Your destiny will have been altered by this dollar. In contrast, suppose you used a dollar for gambling and suffered a loss. Then, because of this loss, you became embroiled in a vicious brawl and landed in jail. Your life would have been ruined by that dollar. Therefore, a dollar is able to determine your destiny.

第二，一句好話可以改變人的命運：

一句好話讚美對方，對方歡喜，給我一些幫助，給我一些建言，從此改變了我的命運；如果一句話說得對方不歡喜，因此開除我，處處刁難我，我的命運可能就此變壞了。

第三，一件善事可以改變人的命運：

我做了一件好事，得了好因好緣，可能就此平步青雲；做了一件壞事，因而惹來災難，麻煩不斷，可能命運就很坎坷了。

第四，一點知識可以改變人的命運：

我有很豐富的知識與技能，除了自受用外，我把它傳授給別人，他因此騰達了，於是回報我，答謝我，我的命運也就跟著改變了。

2. A good word can change your destiny

When a good word is used for praising, it can bring joy to others. Delighted, the others may offer help or good advice in return, thereby changing your destiny. If words are used to upset others, these words may cause others to constantly find fault with you and may even cause you to be dismissed from your job. As a result, your destiny may take a turn for the worse.

3. A good deed can change your destiny

When you do a good deed, plant good seeds, and make good connections, then you can rise to success. If you do a bad deed, you may bring disaster and endless troubles upon yourself. Your life and destiny may then be fraught with difficulties.

4. A little knowledge can change your destiny

Suppose you had a wealth of knowledge and skill. Besides benefiting yourself, you could impart this expertise to another person. Consequently, if this person becomes successful and returns the favor, then your destiny will change.

第五，一些方便可以改變人的命運：

給人方便，就是給自己方便；不給人方便，本來很好的機會也會被破壞而失去，命運就不一樣了。

第六，一個笑容可能改變人的命運：

給人一個微笑，對方很歡喜，會有好緣份。中國民間傳說的「三笑姻緣」，就是一笑訂終身，所以一個笑容，可以決定一個人的命運。

因此，經濟上，一塊錢可以改變我們的命運；語言上，一句好話可以改變我們的命運；功德上，一件善事可以改變我們的命運；教育上，給人一些知識技能可以改變我們的命運；服務上，給人一些方便可以改變我們的命運；面容上，給人

5. A little accommodation can change your destiny

When you accommodate others, you are also accommodating yourself. If you refuse to accommodate or aid others, you may end up missing a wonderful opportunity. Of course, your destiny will be altered.

6. A smile can change your destiny

Give others a smile; it will delight them greatly, and at the same time, help you to make more positive connections. As is said in Chinese folklore, "Three smiles form a matrimonial connection." This means a smile can bind a couple for life. Thus, a smile can also impact your destiny.

In summary, in economic terms, a dollar can change your destiny; in linguistic terms, a good word can change your destiny; merit-wise, a good deed can change your destiny; educationally speaking, imparting knowledge and skills to others can change your destiny; in the field of providing assistance, accom-

一個笑容，都可以改變命運。所以改變命運的是自己本身，因此，大家應該相信命運操之在我，自己改變自己的命運。

如何改變自己的命運？

第一，一塊金錢可以改變人的命運。

第二，一句好話可以改變人的命運。

第三，一件善事可以改變人的命運。

第四，一點知識可以改變人的命運。

第五，一些方便可以改變人的命運。

第六，一個笑容可以改變人的命運。

modating other people's needs can change your destiny; and looking at the area of appearance, a smile can change your destiny. Consequently, each one of us can change our own destiny. We must believe that our destiny is in our own hands.

The following are ways you can change your destiny:

1. A dollar can change your destiny.

2. A good word can change your destiny.

3. A good deed can change your destiny.

4. A little knowledge can change your destiny.

5. A little accommodation can change your destiny.

6. A smile can change your destiny.

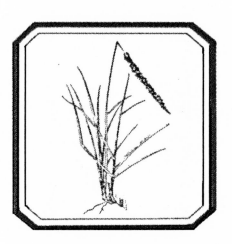

如何做一個善人

我們都希望自己作一個受人尊敬的善人。作一個善人，要有合乎善人的條件。怎麼樣做一個善人呢？我有四點意見：

第一，要修養身心：

所謂修養身心，就是內心清淨光明，身體莊嚴威儀。一舉手、一投足，都讓人覺得很正派。所以修身要非禮勿視、非禮勿聽、非禮勿言、非禮勿動；修心，要把心裡面的骯髒、瞋恨、嫉妒、疑忌都排除。東西髒了，要洗一洗；我們的心髒了，也要把它洗乾淨，所以身心要修養才能清淨，才能正派。

How to be a Good Person

We all hope to be good, well-respected individuals. How do we develop our goodness? I have four suggestions:

1. Cultivate body and mind

Cultivation of body and mind entails comporting oneself with the proper demeanor and maintaining a pure and bright mind. A raising of the hand, a stepping of the foot — all should be conducted with awareness and integrity. Proper cultivation of the body requires seeing no evil, hearing no evil, speaking no evil, and doing no evil. The cultivation of one's mind requires that defilements of the mind, including hatred, jealousy, and suspicion be removed. Dirty things need to be washed; in the same way, a defiled mind needs to be cleaned. Cultivation is necessary for the body and mind to become pure and righteous.

二，要多作善事：

人生苦短，要多作一些慈悲的事、善美的事、有利於別人的事情。作事如果對別人沒有利益，就不合乎慈悲的原則。所以我們要做一些移風易俗、關懷社會、服務人群等有利於大眾的善事。

第三，要敬上念下：

一個善人、好人，對長上要恭敬，對晚輩要愛護。如果對上不敬重，對下不愛護，怎麼能算是一個善人？

第四，要矜恤孤貧：

世界上有很多有錢、有勢、有地位的人，我們不必錦上添花；但是有很多鰥寡孤獨、無依無靠的人，卻需要我們去幫忙。真正的善人，一定會多作矜恤孤貧等雪中送炭的善事。

2. Do good

Because life is limited, one should try to perform many acts of charity, good deeds, and meaningful endeavors. A deed that does not benefit others is not in accordance with the principle of compassion. Therefore, we must strive to improve public morale, to care for society, to serve the masses, and to benefit all people.

3. Respect the elderly and care for the young

A good and kind individual respects the elderly and cares for the young. If one neglects these very basic tasks, how can one be considered a good person?

4. Sympathize and comfort the lonely and the poor

It is not necessary for us to add to what the many rich, powerful, and privileged people of the world already have. It is the lonely, isolated, and deprived who desperately need our assistance. A truly good human being will provide the needy with timely assistance.

怎麼樣做一個善人？有四點：

第一，要修養身心。

第二，要多作善事。

第三，要敬上念下。

第四，要矜恤孤貧。

To become a good individual, we adhere to the following four points:

1. Cultivate body and mind.
2. Do good.
3. Respect the elderly and care for the young.
4. Sympathize and comfort the lonely and the poor.

如何與人相處（一）

How to Get Along With People (I)

人與人相處之道，看起來很難。但下列四點意見只要你做到以後，必能受益無窮：

Getting along with people can be difficult. How do we get along with others? Let me suggest four guidelines. If we can truly practice according to the following guidelines, we should all be able to reap boundless benefits.

第一，你好我壞。

第二，你對我錯。

第三，你大我小。

第四，你有我無。

1. You are good, I am bad.

2. You are right, I am wrong.

3. You are big, I am small.

4. You have, I do not.

在一般人的觀念裡，都不喜歡你好我壞。但如果我什麼都好，別人都壞，人家會饒我嗎？所以，有時讓別人做好人，我當壞人，反而能獲得別人的同情與好感。

When entangled in a dispute, many people dislike the notion, "You're good and I'm bad," but prefer "I'm good and you're bad." Now, suppose that I insist that I am indeed always good, while others are always bad. Would others want to befriend me or forgive my mistakes? Sometimes letting others be good guys while I play the bad guy, on the contrary, will enhance sympathy and good feelings between us.

比方說，有兩戶人家，張姓人家經常吵架，李姓人家卻是

Let me illustrate with one example about two families: The

相安無事、和樂融融。張家因此問李家的人，是什麼原因使家裡能不發生爭吵？李家回答說：因為你們家都是好人，所以吵架；我們家人都是壞人，因而不吵架。

為什麼呢？舉個例子說：桌上放了一個茶杯，張家有人打破了，他不承認自己錯誤，反而責怪放茶杯的人；同樣地，放茶杯的人也說：茶杯是我放的，誰叫你打破了？全家人都要做好人，都不承認自己錯誤，因此就爭吵不休了。

李家的人則都自願做壞人，打破的人立刻就說：「對不起！對不起！是我不小心把茶杯打破了。」而放茶杯的人也會說：「不能怪你，是我不應該把茶杯放在桌上。」

Zhang family was always fighting, while the Li family was peaceful and harmonious. The Zhang family asked the Li family how they prevented their family members from fighting. The Li family replied, "Your family has only good guys so you fight. Our family has only bad guys, therefore, we don't fight."

Why? Let's look at the following scenario. If someone in the Zhang family were to break a teacup left on the table, he would not acknowledge his own mistake. He would lay the blame on the person who had left the teacup there. Similarly, the person who placed the teacup would say: "Sure, I put the teacup there, why did you break it?" The whole family wanted to be good guys; all were reluctant to take the blame. Therefore, they argued endlessly.

However, members of the Li family were all willing to be bad guys. A Li family member, who broke a teacup in such a manner, would immediately say, "Sorry! Sorry! I'm the one who carelessly broke the teacup." And the person who had left the teacup would also say, "It is not your fault; I shouldn't have left the teacup on the table."

In this way, everyone in the Li family was willing to acknowledge his or her own mistakes, and they did not quarrel. In short, if we can practice, "You're good, I'm bad", then many conflicts and problems can be avoided

Similarly, one can also practice: you're right, I'm wrong; you're big, I'm small; you have, I don't have. It may seem very difficult to put these ideas into practice, but if we do, we may be surprised to find many hidden benefits. If we use these suggestions, we will be able to have more harmonious relationships with people.

如此一來，李家的每個人都願意承認自己的錯誤，所以也就不吵架。總之，如能做到你好我壞，便可解決很多的紛爭與問題。

此外，你好我壞，你對我錯，你大我小，你有我無，看起來似乎很難實行，實際上，只要你去實踐，就能發現其中蘊藏了許多微妙的道理，而在人我相處中，你一定會因為以上的幾項方法，而與人相處更融洽。

如何與人相處（二）

人是群居的動物，在家庭裡有父母兄弟，學校裡有老師同學，機關裡有長官同事，街道上人和人摩肩擦踵，所以不管你走到哪裡，總離不開人群。在人群中如何與人和睦相處，有四句話供大家參考：

第一，忍一句，禍根從此無生處：

古德說：「喜時之言多失信，怒時之言多失禮。」一個人在盛怒時所說的話，容易傷害到別人，也容易造成磨擦，所以如果我們能忍一時之氣，就不會造成無謂的紛爭。就像拳頭，不要急著打出去，才能凝聚力量；眼淚，不要輕易流出來，才是真正的悲憤。一時的氣話往往造成不堪設想的後果，因此千萬不要在盛氣之下輕易發言，能忍一句，自然禍

How to Get Along With People (II)

People are social beings. Parents and children make up a family. Teachers and classmates form a school. Supervisors and co-workers interact in the workplace. On the street, people crowd each other shoulder to shoulder. No matter where we go, we will always encounter other people. How can we deal harmoniously with the people we meet? Four sayings are offered here for your consideration:

1. Hold back negative words; there will be no ground in which disaster can grow

There is a saying: "Words spoken during exuberant moments are likely to be unreliable. Words uttered during angry moments are likely to be discourteous." Words that a person says in extreme anger can easily hurt others and induce conflict. Therefore, if we can endure momentary anger in silence, we will not induce unnecessary arguments. Take a fist as an example. If we do not use it hastily, its power will have more force. The same is true for tears.

根從此無生處。

第二，饒一著，切莫與人爭強弱：

　有首偈語說：「何必爭強來鬥勝，百千渾是戲文場；頃刻一聲鑼鼓歇，不知何處是家鄉。」人生就像一場戲，儘管劇中曾經風光、繁華過，一旦落幕，一切歸於寂靜。所以在人生的舞台上實在沒有什值得爭強好勝的，有時候讓人一步就是自己的勝利，所以做人要有「得饒人處且饒人」的涵養與心量。

If we do not shed tears readily, then when we do, we demonstrate our true grief and sorrow. An angry word frequently brings unimagined consequences. Therefore, never speak hurriedly, especially when extremely angry. If one can hold back a hateful word, there will be no place for disaster to take root.

2. Forgive an attack; never fight others for power

A gatha verse states: "Why bother to fight for the upper hand, hundreds and thousands of acts are all but a stage play; once the gongs and the drums cease beating, do you know where your true home is?" Human life is just like a stage play. There may be exuberance in the play, but once the curtain drops, all will return to silence. Therefore, on the stage of life, there really is nothing worth fighting for. Sometimes giving up the lead to others is a victory for oneself. We need to discipline ourselves to have hearts of forgiveness, so that we may "forgive others as much as possible, just as we would forgive ourselves."

第三，耐一時，火坑變作白蓮池：

忍，不是懦弱的表示；忍，是勇者的象徵。一個人能夠忍耐一時，堅持下去，縱使一時的不如意，終將成為過去。縱然處身「火坑」，也會因你的忍耐而變成清涼的蓮池。所以我們與人相處，只要能忍耐，就能轉逆境為順境。

第四，退一步，便是人生修行路：

人生的旅途上，不一定要每一步都向前。回頭是岸，能退一步想，海闊天空；凡事退一點，不但留給人一點餘地，也是自己的一種修行。

3. Endure for a moment; a fiery inferno will turn into a cool lotus pond

Endurance is not a show of cowardice; endurance is a quality of the brave. If one can endure and persevere, then even moments of disappointment will fade into the past. With endurance, even an "inferno of flames" can turn into a clear, cool lotus pond. Therefore, when we deal with people, if we can endure, we can turn an adverse situation into a favorable one.

4. Take a step back; that is the way of self-cultivation

On the journey of life, not every step must be forward. If we can take a step back to reflect, our horizon will be broadened. Stepping back a little in all matters not only leaves others some space, but also advances one's self-cultivation.

所以，與人和諧相處的方法是：

第一，忍一句，禍根從此無生處。

第二，饒一著，切莫與人爭強弱。

第三，耐一時，火坑變作白蓮池。

第四，退一步，便是人生修行路。

Therefore, the ways to deal harmoniously with people are as follows:

1. Hold back negative words; there will be no ground in which disaster can grow.

2. Forgive an attack; never fight others for power.

3. Endure for a moment; a fiery inferno will turn into a cool lotus pond.

4. Take a step back; that is the way of self-cultivation.

如何做一個
正當的人

人活在世間上，如果被別人批評說：「那個人不正派、不正當。」那真是很難為情的事。怎麼樣才能做個正當的人呢？

第一，正當的行為：
做事要正大光明、胸襟要寬大磊落，不可以專做一些偷雞摸狗的事，譬如竊盜、搶劫、綁票等不正當的行為。所以要做個正當的人，先要從正當的行為著手。

第二，正當的語言：
五戒中的妄語、兩舌、惡口、綺語等，都是不正當的語言，都會讓我們成為不受歡迎的人。所以不要妄語，不要說謊，不要綺語，不要隨便說一些不乾不淨的話，所有出之於口的語言，都很正當。

How to Be
a Righteous Person

It is really quite an embarrassment for a person to hear others talking about him or her as being improper and unrighteous. How then can a person become proper and righteous?

1. Righteous behavior
One must behave with a sense of fairness and justice, with an open and impartial mind. One should not engage in cheating and stealing or other aggressions such as burglary, robbery, and kidnapping. To be a righteous person, one must start with righteous behavior.

2. Righteous speech
One of the Five Precepts is to abstain from false words, slander, harsh language, and idle remarks. These types of speech are examples of the unrighteous use of language. They will make us unwelcome in society. Therefore, one must not exaggerate, tell lies, make improper remarks, or use foul language. One must only use righteous language.

66

第三，正當的做人：

我們做人，寧可正派而不足，不可邪惡而有餘；寧可沒有用，沒有能力，也不要被人家批評說：「這個人不正當！」所以做人要正正當當，要正派做人。

第四，正當的處世：

我們和人相處，要給人感覺我不會欺負他，我不會算計他，我不會隨便傷害他。我的所作所為都是正正當當的，正當行事，才能予人安全感。所以我們交朋友，和人相處，先看他為人正當不正當，不一定選擇他地位有多高，財力有多雄厚，或是多麼會說笑，多麼聰明，多麼幹練等條件。有的人聰明、能幹，但是行為不正當，這種人還是一無可取。所以我們跟人相處，要看對方是不是正正當當的做人，這很要緊！

3. Righteous conduct

We should strive to conduct ourselves in a righteous manner, even when we cannot do so perfectly. Under no circumstances should we do evil just because it is the easier choice. It is better to be referred to as "incompetent" or "incapable" than to be judged as an "unrighteous" person. Therefore, we must act in a righteous manner toward others.

4. Righteous dealings

When we deal with someone, we must let the person know that we will not take advantage of him or her, that we will not trick or hurt the person. Our negotiations should be conducted in a correct and righteous manner. Only fair dealings can make people feel secure. So when we make friends and deal with others, it is more important to make sure that the other party is righteous rather than selecting friends on the basis of how important, wealthy, articulate, sociable, smart, and capable they are. Some people are smart and capable but are not righteous; they are not beneficial to others. Therefore, when we deal with someone, we must observe whe-

67

如何做一個正正當當的人呢？
要有：

第一，正當的行為。

第二，正當的語言。

第三，正當的做人。

第四，正當的處世。

ther that person acts righteously. This is very important!

To be a righteous person we must have the following:

1. Righteous behavior.

2. Righteous speech.

3. Righteous conduct.

4. Righteous dealings.

如何認識益友和損友

How to Recognize Beneficial or Destructive Friends

世間上每個人都需要朋友。朋友有所謂的益友與損友。什麼叫益友，什麼又是損友呢？在佛經裡說朋友有四品，就是四種朋友：

In this world, everyone needs friends; however, there are beneficial friends and destructive friends. Who are the beneficial friends, and who are the destructive friends? Buddhist scripture says that there are four kinds of friends. The first two kinds of friends listed below are unhealthy friends, and the last two are healthy friends.

第一，有友如花：

有的朋友像花一樣，當你盛開的時候，他把你插在頭上，供在桌子上；假如你凋謝了，他就把你丟棄。也就是說，當你擁有權勢、富貴的時候，他把你捧得高高的，凡事奉承你、隨順你；一旦你功名富貴沒有了，失去了利用的價值，他就背棄你，離開你，這是嫌貧愛富的朋友。

1. There are friends who treat you like flowers

Some friends treat you like flowers. When you are in full bloom, they wear you on their heads or display you on their tables. When you have withered, they just abandon you. In other words, when you have power and wealth, they praise you and do everything to please and honor you. Once you lose your high status, they will abandon you. These are the kind of friends who reject the poor and praise the rich.

第二，有友如秤：

有的朋友像秤一樣。如果你比他重，他就低頭；如果你比他輕，他就高起來。也就是說，當你有辦法、有名位、有權力時，他就卑躬屈膝、阿諛諂媚的向你低頭；等到你功名權力沒有了，他就昂起頭來，看不起你了。以上兩種是不好的朋友。

另外還有兩種好的朋友：

第三，有友如山：

有的朋友像高山一樣，山能廣植森林，豢養一切飛禽走獸，任憑動物聚集在裡面，自由自在的生活。所以好朋友像山，有著廣闊的心胸，就像孟嘗君一樣，有食客三千，能容納很多的朋友。

第四，有友如地：

有一種朋友如大地，大地能普載萬物，我們在大地上建房子，栽種花草樹木，乃至人、

2. There are friends who act like a scale

Some friends are similar to a scale. If you weigh more than them, they hand their heads low. If you weigh less than them, they stand high above. In other words, when you have resources, fame, and power, they will bend to humble themselves and flatter you. When you have lost your fame and power, they raise their heads high and look down upon you.

3. There are friends who are like mountains

Some friends are like mountains. Mountains sustain the growth of forests, support the lives of fowl and beasts, and allow creatures to congregate and live freely. Therefore, a good friend is like a mountain: he or she has a broad and supportive mind. Like Meng Changjun, who entertained three thousand guests, a good friend can accomodate many, many friends.

4. There are friends who are like the earth

Some friends are like the great earth. The earth contains all

車行走其上，大地都毫無怨尤的承受著。所以，像大地的朋友，可以普載我們，替我們擔當，替我們服務，這兩種如山如地的朋友都是益友。

creatures. We build houses and plant flowers, grass, and trees on the earth. Even with all the people walking and the cars running, the earth receives them without complaint. Therefore, friends who are like the great earth can carry us, share our burdens, and assist us with their services. Friends who are like mountains or the earth are beneficial friends.

所以，大家如何認識益友和損友，就是：

第一，有友如花。

第二，有友如秤。

第三，有友如山。

第四，有友如地。

To help distinguish destructive friends from beneficial ones, just remember to look for the following qualities:

1. Friends who treat you like flowers.
2. Friends who act like a scale.
3. Friends who are like mountains.
4. Friends who are like the earth.

如何不侵犯

做人要厚道，要有愛心，要有慈悲心。什麼叫作愛心和慈悲心呢？能夠不侵犯別人，便是最大的愛心與最大的慈悲心。

如何做到不侵犯？有下列四點：

第一，不為討便宜而侵犯別人：

不侵犯的意思，就是不要為了自己的利益而去傷害別人。比方說：看到別人花園裡盛開的花朵，我就隨意摘幾朵；別人放在桌上的紙、筆，順手拿來就塗塗寫寫；或是任意佔用他人的位置。這些全是為己身的利益、方便而侵犯別人，這就是沒有愛心、沒有慈悲心的侵犯。

第二，不為逞己快而諷刺別人：

有的人為了逞自己一時之快，常常譏諷、嘲笑別人，這是很

How Not to Infringe Upon Others

When dealing with people, one must be sincere, loving, and compassionate. What do the words love and compassion mean? Not infringing upon others is the greatest form of love and compassion.

How can one keep from infringing upon others? The following are four major points:

1. Don't infringe upon others for the purpose of one's own advantage

Not to infringe upon others means not to hurt anyone for one's own benefit. Examples include picking others' blooming flowers for your own pleasure, using others' paper and pen left on the desk, or occupying another's seat at will. These acts all infringe upon others for one's own benefit. These are invasions without love and compassion.

2. Don't tease others for one's own pleasure

Some people often tease or make fun of others for a momen-

缺德的行為。俗語說「禍從口出，病從口入」，不要讓自己的一時之快傷了人，讓不經意的一句話留下終生的憾恨，實在得不償失。

tary pleasure. This is very inconsiderate behavior. It is commonly said: "Troubles come forth from the mouth, diseases enter via the mouth." Don't seek momentary gratification at the expense of others. To have a mindless word cause life-long damage is really an irreparable loss.

第三，不為忌彼好而打擊別人：

人類文化博大精深，歷史悠久，但卻隱藏了見不得別人比自己好的劣根性與嫉妒的心理，所以我們應該開闊心胸，不要看不得他人好而眼紅，去打擊別人。

3. Don't attack others out of jealousy over their better conditions

Our world has a rich, deep, and long history. However, some of us have a tendency to be envious of others who surpass us. Therefore, we must have open minds and not attack others out of jealousy over their better conditions.

第四，不為護私欲而傷害別人：

如果只是為了滿足個人的欲望，不惜傷害別人，這是不道德的行為。

4. Don't hurt others to indulge one's own selfish desires

It is immoral to hurt others to satisfy one's personal desires.

因

此，具足愛心、慈悲心，最重要的是不要傷害他人，不要侵犯他人。慈悲心的表現，愛心的顯露，是四種不侵犯：

第一，不為討便宜而侵犯別人。
第二，不為逞己快而諷刺別人。
第三，不為忌彼好而打擊別人。
第四，不為護私欲而傷害別人。

We should have love and compassion for others. Most of all, we should not hurt and infringe upon others by following these guidelines:

1. Don't infringe upon others for the purpose of one's own advantage.
2. Don't tease others for one's own pleasure.
3. Don't attack others out of jealousy over their better conditions.
4. Don't hurt others to indulge one's own selfish desires.

四種忍 / Four Kinds of Endurance

人間最大的力量不是槍炮、子彈，不是拳頭、武力，人間最大的力量是「忍」。任何力量在忍者的面前，都要甘拜下風。忍有四種真義：

The greatest power in the human world is not guns, bullets, fists, or violence. The greatest power is endurance. All other powers surrender to endurance, of which there are four kinds:

第一，遭惡罵時默而不報：

有人對我們惡口毀謗、無理謾罵時，我們要默而不報，用沉默來對待。不要他惡口罵你，你也回罵他，這樣將會被譏為半斤八兩；如果我們默不作聲，以沉默來折服惡口，讓對方良心甦醒，力量自然更大。

1. Endure verbal attacks without responding

When somebody uses abusive language toward us or scolds us unreasonably, we should deal with it in silence. Do not respond to a person's bad language with bad language, for that would be equally wrong. If we refrain from retorting and let the other person calm down and become reasonable, our power to control the situation naturally becomes greater.

第二，遇打擊時心能平靜：

遇到他人打擊我們、欺負我們時，我們要心平氣和的對待他，不要他打你一拳，你也還他一拳；他踢你一腳，你也還他一腳，這樣誰也不比誰高尚。如果只是爭一時之氣，將

2. Endure physical attacks with calmness

When someone picks on us, or even attacks us, we should deal with that person calmly. Do not return violence with violence, for that will not make either person a winner. Sometimes, when we insist on getting the upper hand for

78

贏不了千秋事業。

a moment, we end up losing the entire endeavor over the long run.

第三，受嫉恨時以慈對待：

假如有人懷恨我們、嫉妒我們，我們不要同樣的以懷恨、嫉妒來對待他，要以慈悲心來待他，要對他更加的友愛，更加的和平，這樣就表示你的修養、力量超越了他。

3. Endure hatred with compassion

If somebody hates us or becomes jealous of us, we should not return that hatred or jealousy. We should deal with him or her with compassion, be more friendly, and be extra calm. This will show your cultivation and that your power of endurance can overcome his or her hatred.

第四，有毀謗時感念其德：

假如有人譏諷我們、毀謗我們，我們不要氣惱他，反而要感念他以往對我們的恩德。尤其要想到，愈是骯髒的污泥愈能生長出清淨的蓮花；越是黑暗的地方，更要點亮心靈的燈光。因此，面對毀謗時，更應該以道德、慈悲心去感化他，如此也愈能彰顯自己的道德、涵養。

所以一個真正的忍者，對待惡罵、打擊、毀謗，都要有承擔、忍耐的力量。忍的力量，勝過一切拳頭刀槍。

4. Endure humiliation with appreciation

If someone taunts us or slanders us, we should not become angry. Instead, we should remember with appreciation any favors he or she has done for us in the past. Most importantly, we should remember that the filthier the mud is, the better the lotus blossoms grow; the darker a place is, the more we should brighten the light in our minds. Therefore, when facing humiliation, use moral strength and compassion to influence others. This will clearly demonstrate one's own good character.

A person with true endurance

has the power to deal with verbal and physical attacks, hatred, and humiliation. The power of endurance can overcome all violence and all types of weapons.

忍有四種真義：

第一，遭惡罵時默而不報。

第二，遇打擊時心能平靜。

第三，受嫉恨時以慈對待。

第四，有毀謗時感念其德。

Again, the four kinds of endurance are as follows:

1. Endure verbal attacks without responding.
2. Endure physical attacks with calmness.
3. Endure hatred with compassion.
4. Endure humiliation with appreciation.

拒絕的藝術

「拒絕」是一種藝術。當別人對你有所希求而你辦不到時，你不得不拒絕他。拒絕是很難堪的，不得已要拒絕的時候，我建議大家一些拒絕的藝術：

第一，不要立刻就拒絕：
立刻拒絕，會讓人覺得你是一個冷漠無情的人，甚至覺得你對他有成見。

第二，不要輕易的拒絕：
有時候輕易的拒絕別人，會失去許多幫助別人、獲得友誼的機會。

第三，不要盛怒下拒絕：
盛怒之下拒絕別人，容易在語言上傷害別人，讓人覺得你一點同情心都沒有。

第四，不要隨便的拒絕：
太隨便地拒絕，別人會覺得你

The Art of Saying "NO"

How to say "No" and how to refuse others tactfully is a skillful art. When others ask us to do something that we cannot deliver, we have no choice but to refuse. However, it is hard to refuse others. I offer here some suggestions on how to decline others when we absolutely must:

1. Do not decline immediately

If we turn others down immediately, it can give others the impression that we are cold and have preconceived notions about them.

2. Do not decline recklessly

When we turn down others recklessly, we can lose many opportunities to help others and to make friends.

3. Do not decline angrily

When we refuse others angrily, we can hurt others' feelings and make them think that we are unsympathetic.

4. Do not decline callously

When we refuse others callously, they may feel slighted,

並不重視他，容易造成反感。

第五，不要無情的拒絕：

無情的拒絕就是表情冷漠，語氣嚴峻，毫無通融的餘地，會令人很難堪，甚至反目成仇。

第六，不要傲慢的拒絕：

一個盛氣凌人、態度傲慢不恭的人，任誰也不會喜歡親近他。何況當他有求於你，而你以傲慢的態度拒絕，別人更是不能接受。

第七，要能婉轉的拒絕：

真正有不得已的苦衷時，如能委婉的說明，以婉轉的態度拒絕，別人還是會感動於你的誠懇。

第八，要有笑容的拒絕：

拒絕的時候，要能面帶微笑，態度要莊重，讓別人感受到你對他的尊重、禮貌，就算被你拒絕了，也能欣然接受。

第九，要有代替的拒絕：

你跟我要求的這一點我幫不上

which in turn can create bad feelings among all.

5. Do not decline cold-heartedly

When we refuse others cold-heartedly, without any room to negotiate, it can embarrass others and can possibly turn them into enemies.

6. Do not decline arrogantly

No one wants to be close to one who is arrogant and disrespectful to others. It is especially hard to accept when someone really needs our help and we arrogantly turn this person down .

7. Decline tactfully

When we really cannot deliver what others ask of us, we should turn them down tactfully. In this way, they will be touched by our sincerity and truthfulness.

8. Decline with a smile

When we refuse others, it is important that we act friendly and with respect. This allows others to maintain their dignity and accept our refusal more easily.

9. Decline with an alternative

If we cannot help others when they ask us for help, suggest an

忙，我用另外一個方法來幫助你，這樣一來，他還是會很感謝你的。

alternative way that we can help them. In this way, they will be thankful for our thoughtfulness.

第十，要有出路的拒絕：

拒絕的同時，如果能提供其他的方法，幫他想出另一條出路，實際上還是幫了他的忙。

10. Decline with a solution

Although we may not be able to help a person when he asks us for help, we can offer him a solution. When we do this, we are indirectly helping him.

第十一，要有幫助的拒絕：

也就是說你雖然拒絕了，但卻在其他方面給他一些幫助，這是一種慈悲而有智慧的拒絕。

11. Decline helpfully

Even though we may not be able to help him in a particular instance, we may be able to help him in some other way. This shows wisdom and compassion on our part.

所以，拒絕要有藝術，要能：

第一，不要立刻就拒絕。

第二，不要輕易的拒絕。

第三，不要盛怒下拒絕。

第四，不要隨便的拒絕。

第五，不要無情的拒絕。

第六，不要傲慢的拒絕。

In summary, the following are important ways to decline others skillfully:

1. Do not decline immediately.

2. Do not decline recklessly.

3. Do not decline angrily.

4. Do not decline callously.

5. Do not decline cold-heartedly.

6. Do not decline arrogantly.

第七，要能婉轉的拒絕。　　　　7.　Decline tactfully.

第八，要有笑容的拒絕。　　　　8.　Decline with a smile.

第九，要有代替的拒絕。　　　　9.　Decline with an alternative.

第十，要有出路的拒絕。　　　　10.　Decline with a solution.

第十一，要有幫助的拒絕。　　　11.　Decline helpfully.

如何和諧相處

How to Live in Harmony with Each Other

人與人之間要互相尊重，如果你看不起別人，或別人不尊重你，彼此就不能和諧相處。人與人和諧相處之道有四：

第一，彼此尊重：

有一天，眉毛、眼睛、鼻子、嘴巴在開會，眼睛、鼻子、嘴巴都認為眉毛最沒有用，怎麼可以高高在上？大家你一言我一句，說得眉毛招架不住，只好自願移到下面來。但是不管移到眼睛、鼻子或嘴巴的下面，都不成人形，最後只好還是讓眉毛高居上位。所以人與人之間要彼此尊重，才能互相幫助，互得利益。

People must respect one another. If you do not respect others, or if others are prejudiced against you, it will be impossible to live together in harmony. The following are four ways to live together in harmony:

1. Respect one another

One day, the eyebrows, eyes, nose, and mouth became involved in a discussion. The eyes, nose, and mouth felt that the eyebrows were the least useful, and wondered how they could be situated in the highest position on the face. The debate became very heated, with each criticizing the other. Finally, in an attempt to end the debate, the eyebrows volunteered to relocate to a lower position. However, no matter where the eyebrows went, below the eyes, nose, or mouth, the face looked ridiculous. Finally, all agreed to allow the eyebrows to return to their original position. Thus, people must respect each other's position, help each other, and work together so everyone benefits. In this way, mutual respect will be achieved.

第二，樂善好施：

佛教講「無緣大慈，同體大悲」。我們對於任何人，都要給人幾句好話的布施，給人一個微笑的布施，給人一個點頭的布施，因為唯有對人尊敬，給人一點助力，才能獲得友誼。

第三，心理健康：

人和人相處，如果常常心存懷疑，別人講一句話，你就認為是在批評你；別人做一件事，你就擔心可能對自己不利。如此多疑、善嫉，將會失去很多的友誼。因此，要心理健康，要對人信賴，對人友好，對人放心，才能和人相處愉快。

第四，互相幫助：

有一個趣談指出天堂和地獄的不同：地獄的人吃飯用的筷子

2. Be kind and generous to others

Buddhism teaches: "Be kind to everyone without any cause; be compassionate as we all are one." When we deal with others, we need to be generous with our compliments and give warm smiles and acknowledgments. Only by respecting and helping others can one gain friendship.

3. Maintain psychological health

We live and deal with one another on a daily basis. If we are suspicious, then whenever someone says anything, we automatically think they are criticizing us, or when someone does something to us, we think of it as being unfavorable and that we are being taken advantage of. Such suspicion and defensiveness will cause us to lose many friendships. Therefore, for our psychological health, we must trust others, be friendly, and open our minds so that we can live happily and harmoniously.

4. Provide mutual assistance

There is a joke about the difference between heaven and hell. It is said that people in hell use

有三尺長，夾了菜還來不及送到自己嘴裡，便給鄰座的人搶去吃了，因此便互相責怪對方。天堂裡的人吃飯用的筷子也是三尺長，不過他們夾了菜以後是互相送給對方吃，對方也是如此。由於彼此互相尊重、互相幫助、互相友愛，因此，天堂裡永遠充滿和諧、快樂的氣氛。

所以，人和人如何相處呢？

第一，彼此尊重。
第二，樂善好施。
第三，心理健康。
第四，互相幫助。

three-foot long chopsticks to eat. It is impossible to put the food into their mouths because the persons next to them snatch the food away. They end up arguing among themselves. Therefore, everyone is starving. People in heaven also use three-foot long chopsticks to eat. But there they feed the person across from them so that everyone is able to eat his or her fill. Because of respect, help, and friendliness, heaven is filled with an atmosphere of harmony and happiness.

Therefore, how can we live together in harmony?

1. Respect one another.
2. Be kind and generous to others.
3. Maintain psychological health.
4. Provide mutual assistance.

處理是非的方法

有人說：「有人的地方就有是非。」是非雖然到處可見，不過所謂「是非朝朝有，不聽自然無」，只要我們懂得處理是非，自然不會受其干擾。

處理是非的方法，有下列四點：

第一，不說是非：
俗語說：「謠言止於智者」。再多的謠言、是非，只要我不說，是非自然消失。

第二，不傳是非：
我不但不說是非，而且面對是非，要做到不傳播是非，以免是非渲染、擴大。

第三，不理是非：
對於世間的是是非非，你愈理它，它就愈理愈亂。所以處理是非的另一個辦法是，不理是非。

Ways of Handling Gossip

Someone once said: "Where there are people, there is gossip." Even though gossip can be everywhere, we should keep the following in mind: "Gossip arises day after day; don't listen, then it goes away." If we know how to handle gossip, we won't be bothered by it.

The following are four ways of handling gossip:

1. Don't gossip
It is commonly said: "Rumors stop at the wise person." No matter how many rumors I hear, if I don't pass them along they will naturally fizzle and disappear.

2. Don't spread gossip
Do not start gossip and do not spread it around. In this way, gossip will not be amplified and no one will be harmed by it.

3. Don't deal with gossip
The more you deal with gossip, the messier it becomes. Therefore, the best way to deal with gossip is simply to ignore it.

第四，不聽是非：

儘管再多的是非，我都「非禮勿聽」，因為是非、謠言是極可怕的。對日抗戰期間，有一天，空襲警報聲大作，有個人說：「一架飛機來襲了！」隨後有人問：「多少飛機啊？」他回答：「是一架飛機！」問的人沒聽清楚，就立刻傳告別人：「十一架飛機！」有人再問多少架飛機，他說：「就是一架飛機。」結果謠傳到最後成為「九十一架飛機」，可見以訛傳訛，多手傳播的可怕。

4. Don't listen to gossip

Although gossip abounds everywhere, I always "hear no evil" because gossip and rumors are terrible. One day, during the war against the Japanese, the air raid siren sounded loudly. Someone said, "An air raid is coming!" Then another person asked, "How many airplanes?" He replied, "There is one airplane!" The one who asked did not listen carefully and immediately said to others, "Eleven airplanes!"* When other people asked again about the number of planes, the first man said, "There indeed is one airplane!" The rumor ended up as "ninety-one airplanes."** As you can see, falsehood can spread like wild fire. Rumors exaggerate the situation and bring confusion and fear.

* "Is one" and "eleven" are homonyms in Chinese. They are both pronounced "Shi Yi."
** "Indeed is one" and "ninety-one" are homonyms in Chinese. They are both pronounced "Jiu Shi Yi."

因此，我們要想過清淨自在的
生活，就要會處理是非。處理
是非的方法有：

第一，不說是非。
第二，不傳是非。
第三，不理是非。
第四，不聽是非。

Therefore, if we want to lead
pure and free lives, we must
know how to deal with gossip.
Again four ways to handle gossip are as follows:

1. Don't gossip.
2. Don't spread gossip.
3. Don't deal with gossip.
4. Don't listen to gossip.

鋪好行為平坦的道路

一個人的一生，其幸福決定於自己的行為，至於未來生活好或不好，不是另外有神明來懲罰我們或賞賜我們，這全是我們自己所招感的。所謂身、口、意的業力，發之於行為，就會成為果報。那麼，如何鋪好行為平坦的道路，必須作到四點：

第一，要有不犯他人的慈悲：

在倡導自由民主的今日社會中，所謂「自由」，就是不侵犯他人，尊重他人的自由，所以我們尊重別人、愛護別人，不去侵犯別人，就是最大的慈悲。

第二，要有柔和處事的安忍：

我們處事態度，要有柔和的安忍，要用溫柔平和的心、安詳忍耐的力量去看事，去處理事情。

Paving a Steady Path of Behavior

In a person's life, happiness is determined by one's own behavior. Our future is not determined by deities but by ourselves. There are no gods to punish or reward us. The karma of body, speech, and thought carried out through our behavior will result in retribution. Therefore, how do we pave a steady path of behavior? We must do four things:

1. Have the compassion to not violate others

Nowadays, many of us live in a society that promotes freedom and democracy. "Freedom" means to respect each other's liberty and not to violate others. Therefore, the greatest compassion we can express is to show respect to others, to care for others, and not to infringe upon others.

2. Have the endurance to deal with others gently

We should deal with daily matters with forbearance of peaceful endurance. Then we can look at the world with serenity and patience, and handle our matters with a gentle and tranquil mind.

第三，要有勤儉樸實的習慣：

要有正當的勤勞。佛教中有四正勤：未生的惡要令它不生，已生的惡要讓它斷除，已生的善要讓它增長，未生的善要讓它生起。除此之外，還要節儉，節儉不光是財富的節儉、物質的節儉，更是感情的節儉、時間的節儉。一切都要有勤儉樸實的習慣。

3. Have the habit of being diligent and thrifty

We all need to practice right effort. In Buddhism, there are four kinds of right effort: prevent unformed evil from arising, eradicate existing evil, nurture the ongoing good, and bring the unformed good into existence. In addition, we should also be thrifty. The practice of thriftiness is not limited to fortune and material wealth only. This practice also entails economical time management and prudent control of our emotions. In all aspects of life, we should have a habit of being diligent and economical.

第四，要有維護正義的勇氣：

觀世音菩薩還有一個名字，叫作「施無畏」，即布施無畏，讓你不畏懼。給人不畏懼，就是我們要有維護正義的勇氣。

4. Have the courage to protect justice

Avalokitesvara Bodhisattva has another name, "The Bestower of Fearlessness." It means bestowing fearlessness so that others will not be fearful. The giving of fearlessness means that we must have the courage to protect justice.

我們舖好行為平坦的道路，須作到：

第一，要有不犯他人的慈悲。

第二，要有柔和處事的安忍。

第三，要有勤儉樸實的習慣。

第四，要有維護正義的勇氣。

For us to pave a steady path of behavior, we must do the following:

1. Have the compassion not to violate others.
2. Have the endurance to deal with others gently.
3. Have the habit of being diligent and thrifty.
4. Have the courage to protect justice.

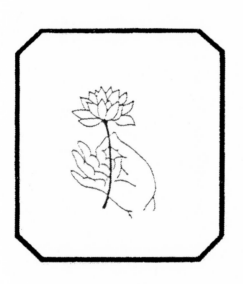

如何美化人生

How to Beautify Human Life

我們常說美化家庭、美化環境、美化社會，要美化這個、美化那個，其實最要緊的是美化自己，美化每一個人的心；美化我們的人生。

如何美化人生呢？

Often we speak about beautifying our families, the environment, society, and so forth. Actually, the most important thing is to beautify oneself, and once that is done, to beautify the minds of everyone. This is beautifying human life.

How do we beautify human life?

第一，美化語言：

語言是人與人溝通的橋樑。我們每天所說的話，如何讓人感到簡潔明瞭，讓人生起歡喜心。尤其要發人深省，增加人的道德，增加人的知識，這就是語言的美化。有的人口中儘說些不好聽的話，甚至說髒話罵人，這就像廁所、糞桶一樣，污穢、骯髒不堪。因此，美化了口舌，語言就能清淨，所以語言的美化很重要。

1. Beautify language

Language is the bridge of communication between human beings. The words we speak should be concise and clear, allowing people to take delight in our conversation. In particular, let us use words to facilitate and encourage introspection, increase morality in the world, and bring about a greater amount of knowledge. This is what is meant by beautifying language. Some people like to say ugly and dirty things. They like to antagonize and use bad language. Their mouths are like toilets — filthy and dirty. When we beautify our speech, the language we use will be clean and pure. Clearly, beautifying our language is very important.

第二，美化面容：

有首偈語說：「面上無瞋是供養」，我們給人一個笑容，這也是一種布施。觀世音菩薩為什麼廣受信徒的尊敬供養？這是因為他能慈眼視眾生，他能給人歡喜。世間最美的就是笑容，我們都希望看到別人給我們笑容，同樣的，我們也要多給別人笑容，所以要時時以微笑來美化面容。

第三，美化行為：

現在社會上流行進修美姿、美儀等課程。這是為了培養自己走路，乃至行儀舉止的優美姿勢，就像演藝人員，他們在舞台上的各種動作也都要講究美感。除肢體動作的美感以外，更要美化自己的行為，所謂美化行為就是不亂殺生、不竊盜、不邪淫，這就是美化行為。

2. Beautify the face

Consider the following verse: "A face showing no anger is a true offering." When we smile at someone, this is also a kind of offering. Why does Avalokitesvara Bodhisattva receive such widespread reverence and offerings from devotees? It is because the Bodhisattva looks at sentient beings with compassionate eyes and delights them with a kind and radiant face. The most beautiful thing in the world is a smile, and we all hope that others will smile at us. Similarly, we should always smile at them. By smiling, we will beautify our faces.

3. Beautify behavior

Nowadays, classes that teach us how to make beautiful gestures and develop good manners are popular. These classes teach us how to walk and act very gracefully, like stage actors and actresses. But, in addition to beautiful body movements, we need to beautify our behavior. Beautiful behavior means abstaining from killing, from stealing, and from sexual misconduct.

第四，美化心理：

高雄縣縣長余陳月瑛曾經推動「心靈淨化運動」，就是要美化心靈，要點亮我們心靈的燈光，清除我們心靈的污垢，建設我們心靈的真、善、美淨土。所謂「心淨則國土淨」，心理能夠淨化，世界自然就能美化，呈現一片清淨、祥和的氣氛。

如何美化人生呢？就是：

第一，美化語言。

第二，美化面容。

第三，美化行為。

第四，美化心理。

4. Beautify the mind

The magistrate of Kaohsiung County, Yu Chen Yueyin, once promoted a program "to purify the mind." The program consisted of beautifying the mind by brightening the light of our minds, cleaning the dust from our minds, and developing in our minds the Pureland of truth, goodness, and beauty. This is the meaning of the statement "When one's mind is pure, the land will be pure." If the mind can be purified, the world will naturally be beautified, and a clean, harmonious atmosphere will arise.

To beautify human life, we must:
1. Beautify language.
2. Beautify the face.
3. Beautify behavior.
4. Beautify the mind.

做什麼樣的人

孔子說：「見賢思齊，見不賢而內自省！」做人，應該為自己樹立學習的榜樣，同時也應該把自己塑造成別人效法的模範。

如何讓自己成聖、成賢呢？我有六點意見：

第一，要像一面鏡子，自我觀照：

一般人都只看得到別人的錯誤，卻看不見自己的缺點，因此需要一面鏡子，從鏡子裡透視自己，觀照自己，改進自己。

第二，要像一只皮箱，提放自如：

皮箱在我們有用時，就將它提起，不用時就把它放下。倘若不用皮箱時，你仍然把它提在手上，便是累贅；反之，要用

What Kind of People should We Be?

Confucius once said, "When we see the virtuous, we should learn from them; when we see the unrespectable, we should reflect on ourselves." We should have exemplary models to guide us on how to conduct ourselves in daily life. At the same time, we should strive to become models of behavior for others.

How does one become virtuous and saintly? I have six suggestions:

1. Like a mirror, reflect upon ourselves

Most people only see the faults of others but never see their own shortcomings. Therefore, we need a mirror to carefully inspect ourselves, to reflect upon ourselves, and to improve ourselves.

2. Like a briefcase, pick up and let go at ease

When we need a briefcase, we pick it up. When we no longer need it, we set it aside. If we hold on to the briefcase when we do not need it, it becomes a burden. On the other hand, if we cannot

時，沒有皮箱，就會有不便之處。所以我們做人要像皮箱一樣，能夠提得起放得下。提所當提，放所當放，提放自如。

find the briefcase when we need it, it is a great inconvenience. Therefore, when we conduct ourselves, we should take ourselves seriously when the circumstances demand it, but let go when the need has passed. In doing this, we will truly feel free.

第三，要像一枝彩筆，彩繪人生：

彩筆可以畫出美麗的山水、動人的圖案；我們做人也要像一支彩筆，彩繪出自己五彩繽紛的美好人生。

3. Like a color pen, beautify and improve life

Color pens can be used to generate beautiful images and impressive pictures. Likewise, we should use our capabilities to enhance our lives, thereby creating a wonderful way to live.

第四，要像一本簿子，記錄功過：

簿子是拿來記事用的。做人也要像一本簿子，要把自己的功過一一記錄下來，做為自我的勉勵與警惕。

4. Like a notebook, record all our successes and failures

A notebook is used for recording purposes. We should conduct ourselves similarly by honestly recording everything we have done, whether successful or otherwise. Then we need to encourage or admonish ourselves accordingly.

第五，要像一枝蠟燭，照亮別人：

　一個人絕不可以自私自利，要經常設身處地的為別人著想。要如同蠟燭一般的「燃燒自己，照亮別人」，這就是我為人人，人人為我的人生哲學。

第六，要像一個時鐘，珍惜生命：

　時鐘從一到十二，每天循序漸進、循規蹈矩的運轉，從不會恣意的由一點跳到五點；也不會永遠停留在某一刻，它很公平的給每個人一天二十四小時，一旦過去了就不再回頭。所以它啟示我們，要及時把握時間，要讓自己的生命作充分的發揮。

5. Like a candle, brighten up others' lives

A person should never be self-centered and selfish. We should always put ourselves in others' circumstances. Just like a candle is burned to illuminate people's lives, we can brighten the lives of others with selfless conduct. This is the foundation of an altruistic philosophy.

6. Like a clock, keep track of and cherish every moment

Every day the clock ticks from one to twelve, turning and advancing in an orderly fashion. It never skips abruptly from one o'clock to five o'clock, nor dwells upon one particular moment. There are twenty-four hours in a day for everybody. Once a day has passed, it will never return. This serves as a reminder for us to cherish every minute, allowing for full realization of our potential.

所以，我們應該做一個像什麼樣的人呢？

第一，要像一面鏡子，自我觀照。
第二，要像一只皮箱，提放自如。
第三，要像一枝彩筆，彩繪人生。
第四，要像一本簿子，記錄功過。
第五，要像一枝蠟燭，照亮別人。
第六，要像一個時鐘，珍惜生命。

Therefore, what kind of people should we be?

1. Like a mirror, reflect upon ourselves.
2. Like a briefcase, pick up and let go at ease.
3. Like a color pen, beautify and improve life.
4. Like a notebook, record all our successes and failures.
5. Like a candle, brighten up others' lives.
6. Like a clock, keep track of and cherish every moment.

我能為世間留下什麼

俗話說：「人死留名，樹死留皮」。人到世間上來走了一趟，是否曾想過，我能為世間留下一些什麼？古人有所謂的三不朽：「立功、立德、立言」。我們如何為世間留下永垂不朽的功德、名聲呢？我有三點意見：

第一，為社會留下建設、發心、奉獻：

所謂建設不一定是什麼大工程，只要有益大眾，比方種幾棵樹，栽一些花，造一座橋，修一條路，乃至留下一個值得紀念的涼亭、欄杆等，都是我們能為社會留下的建設，也代表我們的一份發心、一份奉獻。

What Can I Contribute to the World?

There is a popular Chinese saying: "When a person dies, he leaves behind his name. When a tree dies, it leaves behind its form." When we journey through our lives, do we ever think about what we can do for the world? A famous, ancient proverb says: "Three things are immortal: meritorious deeds, virtues, and noble words." How can we leave a lasting record of virtue and an honorable name to the world? I have three suggestions:

1. Serve society by building, exerting effort, and making positive contributions

"Building" does not mean you have to undertake a spectacular construction project. You only need to do something beneficial for others. For example, we can plant a few trees and some flowers, facilitate the construction of a bridge, help to repair a road, or even erect a memorial gazebo or a safety railing. These examples are all forms of building and signify our efforts and contributions to society.

第二，為朋友留下親切、服務、善緣：

朋友為什麼要和我們交往？一定認為我有益於他，因此我們對朋友要給他一些幫助，要對他有一些影響。我能對朋友有些什麼影響呢？譬如我很親切，我肯為他服務，我留給他一些善緣，讓我所交往的每一個朋友都能得到我的幫助，得到我的利益。

第三，為生命留下信仰、證悟、功德：

人生在世，不過數十寒暑，每個人到頭終難免一死，但死的是有形的軀殼，精神是不死的，只要我有信仰，我有崇高的人格、道德，我有般若、智慧，我的生命將與天地同在，亙古長存。

2. Give warmth, provide service, and maintain good relations with friends

Why do people want to be our friends? Because they feel we benefit them in some way. Therefore, we should offer our friends help and we should be a good influence. How can we be a good influence on our friends? For example, I can be very caring towards them, be of service to them, and have a good relationship with them. By doing so, I can help and benefit every one of my friends.

3. Have religious faith, attain awareness, and accumulate merits in life

A person usually lives in this world for only so many years. Everyone eventually dies. However, death occurs to our physical form, but not to our spirit. If we have religious faith, excellent character, good morals, and wisdom, we will live forever with the universe.

所以，我們能為世間留下什麼？

第一，為社會留下建設、發心、奉獻。
第二，為朋友留下親切、服務、善緣。
第三，為生命留下信仰、證悟、功德。

Therefore, how can I contribute to the world?

1. Serve society by building, exerting effort, and making positive contributions.
2. Give warmth, provide service, and maintain good relations with friends.
3. Have religious faith, attain awareness, and accumulate merits in life.

我們要信仰什麼

In Whom should We Believe?

每一個人活在世間上，除了要求種種的生活方式以外，都須有一個信仰。這個信仰，並沒有宗教上一定的限制，重要的是你不能迷信，不能邪信，更不能誤信。放眼今日社會，信仰錯誤的人比比皆是，究竟我們要信仰什麼呢？

信仰應有如下的條件：

When we live in this world, in addition to pursuing varying lifestyles, we all need to have faith and beliefs. Although beliefs are not limited to religion, it is very important that we do not to harbor superstitious, evil, or delusive beliefs. People with improper beliefs are everywhere. In whom should we believe?

The following points are the criteria of right belief:

第一，信仰實在實有的：

我們信仰的對象，一定要在歷史上有根有據。比方說：釋迦牟尼佛、耶穌基督、穆罕默德、孔子、老子，這些信仰的對象是實在實有的，而非來無影、去無蹤，憑空想像出來的。

1. Believe in those who are real

We should believe in someone who can be substantiated by historical records. For instance, the Buddha, Jesus, Mohammed, Confucius, and Lao Tzu were not fictitious, but real historical figures.

第二，信仰道德高尚的：

我們信仰的對象，其道德是否圓滿？人格是否高尚？身心是否清淨？都是我們所應該深思、了解的。

2. Believe in those who are virtuous

Is our belief rooted in someone whose morals are exemplary, whose character is noble, and whose conduct and thoughts are pure? These issues should be considered and understood fully.

第三，信仰能力強大的：

他具有能力，能救苦救難嗎？如果他連自己都無法挽救，又怎能救我們呢？所以，我們不能信仰一些不明的神仙，因為那種鬼神不能幫助我們獲得解脫，因此不值得信仰。

第四，信仰戒行清淨的：

如果我們信仰的神，要人殺生來祭祀祂，這便是不能清淨戒行，又如何能大慈大悲呢？

第五，信仰正法圓滿的：

信仰的正法如果不能圓滿，處處有缺陷，如何能徹底解決我們面臨的問題呢？

第六，信仰智慧超然的：

有超然的智慧，才能透視生命，才能解決世間、出世間的苦難及煩惱，才是值得我們信仰的。

3. Believe in those who are able

Is our belief rooted in someone who is capable of relieving suffering and helping others? If one is unable to save oneself, how can one help others? Thus, we cannot believe in obscure spirits for they are unable to help us become liberated.

4. Believe in those with pure precepts and practice

If the worship of a deity requires animal sacrifices, then such precepts and practices are far from pure. Under these circumstances, how are we being kind and compassionate?

5. Believe in those with complete and perfect teachings

If we believe in a doctrine that is incomplete and defective in many ways, how can it really help us solve the problems we face?

6. Believe in those who have the wisdom to transcend life

Only those with transcendental wisdom can have a thorough understanding of life. Transcendental wisdom can help us alleviate affliction and distress in the human and supramundane worlds. Therefore, those with transcendental wisdom are worthy of our belief.

所以，我們要信仰什麼？

第一，信仰實在實有的。

第二，信仰道德高尚的。

第三，信仰能力強大的。

第四，信仰戒行清淨的。

第五，信仰正法圓滿的。

第六，信仰智慧超然的。

Therefore, in whom should we believe?

1. Believe in those who are real.
2. Believe in those who are virtuous.
3. Believe in those who are able.
4. Believe in those with pure precepts and practice.
5. Believe in those with complete and perfect teachings.
6. Believe in those who have the wisdom to transcend life.

信仰佛教的意義

「信仰佛教有什麼意義？」時常有人提出這樣的疑問。現在我明白的告訴各位，信仰佛教的意義是：

第一，為生命留下歷史：
　一個人活在世間上，不過短短數十年寒暑，生也好，死也好，大多是庸碌平凡的，無人知道，生來死去都沒留下一點紀念，假如信仰佛教以後，知道了生命的意義，可以為個己的生命留下一個歷史，留下一些紀念。

第二，為社會留下慈悲：
　一個信仰宗教的人，他對社會有責任感，像基督徒講博愛，佛教徒說慈悲，所謂「慈能予樂，悲能拔苦」，信仰佛教的人，要為國家解除困難，給予社會大眾安樂，救濟社會大眾的苦惱，拔除社會大眾的災難。

The Significance of Believing in Buddhism

People often ask, "What is the significance of believing in Buddhism?" My answer to this question is in the form of four suggestions.

1. Live a meaningful life

A person lives in the world for a number of years. Most lead only an ordinary life, remain unknown to others, and leave behind no trace in history. Buddhism can help us to have a better understanding of the meaning of life so that we can lead a life that is significant in history, something that will be remembered.

2. Bring kindness and compassion to society

A religious person carries a sense of responsibility toward society. Christians emphasize love; Buddhists emphasize kindness and compassion. Kindness brings happiness, and compassion eases sorrow. Buddhists should help to resolve national problems, give peace and happiness to the masses of society, and help alleviate affliction and distress.

第三，為自己留下信仰：

信仰佛教的人，常常參加一些佛學講座，參加一些法會，常常到寺院服務，就在道場裡留下了你的信仰。因為一個佛教徒，他的人格、他的道德，都可以從信仰裡看出來，在道場留下自己的信仰，就是留下他的人格、他的道德。

第四，為人間留下貢獻：

一個沒有宗教的人，不容易有視人如己的心胸。如果他有了佛教的信仰，他就會為人間從事很多的慈善事業，對人間做很多的服務，也為人間留下很多的貢獻，使人景仰懷念。

我們信仰佛教的意義，就是：

第一，為生命留下歷史。
第二，為社會留下慈悲。
第三，為自己留下信仰。
第四，為人間留下貢獻。

3. Share one's beliefs

As practicing Buddhists, when we frequently attend lectures on the Buddhist teachings, participate in Dharma functions, and volunteer our services in the temple, we share our spiritual faith with others. Since a Buddhist's character and morals are revealed through his or her beliefs, building faith helps establish character and morals. When we share our faith with others, we are also expressing our character and morals.

4. Give service to the world

A person without religious conviction may not be able to treat others as oneself. If one puts Buddhism into practice, he or she will do many works of charity, provide many services, make many contributions to the world, and will be respected by others.

Believing in Buddhism allows one to do the following:

1. Live a meaningful life.
2. Bring kindness and compassion to society.
3. Share one's beliefs.
4. Give service to the world.

如何祈求

一般的宗教徒，不管是信仰佛教、基督教或是一般的神道教，我想每個人一定都有祈求的經驗。但是要怎樣的祈求才是高貴的祈求呢？我貢獻各位四點意見：

第一，要求神明的感應，更要求內心的體驗：

我們有時候祈求神明給我們富貴平安、吉祥如意、升官發財，這是希求感應，但是我們更應該求內心的體驗。在宗教的信仰裡，內心的體驗比外在的感應更重要，因為我們內心有智慧，有般若，有體驗，有道德，遇到困難的時候就不必假借外面的力量來幫忙我了，所以內心的體驗更重要。

How to Pray

An important question for all religious followers, regardless of whether their faith rests in Buddhism, Christianity or any other religion, is "What is the proper way to pray?" Let me offer four suggestions:

1. Request a response to the prayers, but more importantly, pray for understanding and inner experience

We sometimes pray for wealth, status, peace, fulfillment of our wishes, or career advancement. Instead, we should pray for understanding and inner experience. In religious practice, understanding from within is more important than response from without. When we have intelligence, wisdom, understanding, and morality inside us, we do not need outside help in difficult times. This is why inner experience is most important.

第二，要求自己的平安，更要求大眾的幸福：

一個人只求自己平安，自己好，是不夠的，大眾的幸福、快樂更重要。所以慈航法師說：「只要一人未度，切莫自己逃了。」大家幸福，我才能幸福；大家平安，我才能平安；大家不幸福平安，我也不能幸福平安。

2. Request well-being for oneself, but more importantly, pray for the happiness and well-being of all living beings

It is not enough for a person to pray for one's own well-being; the happiness of all beings is more important. That is why Venerable Cihang said, "Do not attain liberation for oneself if there is even one person left unliberated." When everyone is happy, then I will be happy. When everyone is safe, then I will be safe. When others are not happy or safe, neither am I.

第三，要求世間的富貴，更要求出世的聖財：

世間上的富貴是有限的，出世的聖財是無盡的。比方說：我自己有禪定，有般若智慧，有慚愧心，有懺悔的美德，這比世間上的富貴更重要。

3. Request mundane wealth and status, but more importantly, pray for transcendental wealth

The riches of the world are limited, yet those of transcendence are without bounds. The virtues of meditation, wisdom, humility, and repentance are more important than the wealth of the world.

第四，要求色身的延長，更要求生命的永恆：

一個人不管是活到一百歲、一百二十歲，或者再高的壽命，也仍然是有限的，不如求永恆的生命。所謂永恆的生命就是：立德、立言、立功，這才是不死的生命。

所以，要如何祈求呢？

第一，要求神明的感應，更要求內心的體驗。

第二，要求自己的平安，更要求大眾的幸福。

第三，要求世間的富貴，更要求出世的聖財。

第四，要求色身的延長，更要求生命的永恆。

4. Request longevity of the body, but more importantly, pray for immortality of the spiritual life

A person, even if he or she lives a century or longer, is mortal. Why don't we seek spiritual immortality instead? One can achieve spiritual immortality through meritorious deeds, noble words, and virtues. This is the immortal spiritual life.

Therefore, how should one pray?

1. Request a response to the prayers, but more importantly, pray for understanding and inner experience.
2. Request well-being for oneself, but more importantly, pray for the happiness and well-being of all living beings.
3. Request mundane wealth and status, but more importantly, pray for transcendental wealth.
4. Request longevity of the body, but more importantly, pray for immortality of the spiritual life.

如何廣結善緣 （一）

How to Strengthen Our Affinity with Others (I)

俗話說：「有緣千里來相會，無緣對面不相識。」人和人相遇時常說：「我們有緣。」緣是要靠自己去培植，也就是要廣結善緣。

怎樣和人廣結善緣呢？

It is said, "With affinity, people will meet even if they are thousands of miles apart; without affinity people will remain strangers despite standing face to face." Causal connections are what bring people together. Causal connections need to be cultivated by our own efforts. We should broaden our positive connections with others.

How do we broaden good causal connections with others?

第一，用經濟結緣：

所謂經濟結緣就是物質、金錢上的結緣，譬如我給你一根針、一條線，甚至於一塊麵包，我就跟你結了緣。

1. Form connections through the economy

Economic connections are formed through materialistic and monetary means. For example, if I give you a sewing needle, a strand of thread, or a slice of bread, I have formed a causal connection with you through the economy.

第二，用語言結緣：

對人說一句好話，讚美別人，這種語言上的結緣往往產生不可思議的效果，只是一句好話，卻結下了生生世世不解的善因善緣。

2. Form connections through speech

To form speech connections is to say nice words to others and to praise others. The effects of forming such connections can reach far beyond one's imagination. A few nice words may form a good cause and a good connection that transcend one's lifetime, even into many future lifetimes.

第三，用功德結緣：

功德結緣就是做善事。譬如修橋、舖路，熱心社會公益等，這就是功德結緣。

3. Form connections through merits

Forming meritorious connections is achieved through doing good deeds. When one helps with tasks, such as building bridges and paving roads, or is involved in other beneficial community activities, one forms connections with others through merit.

第四，用教育結緣：

我傳授你技術，告訴你怎樣做好人，如何做好事，就是教育結緣。尤其今日的社會，學校的青年學子吸食安非他命，實在是戕害身心，如果老師、家長，甚至朋友、同學，能勸誡他不要再吸食安非他命，引導他走向正途，日後他可能會對我們心存感激。

4. Form connections through education

When we teach others technical skills, teach them how to be good people, or how to perform good deeds, we form causal connections with them through education. The educational connection is particularly important in today's society where substance abuse is rampant in our school system and young people are damaging their bodies and minds by using illicit drugs. If teachers, parents, friends, and classmates advise a student not to use illicit substances and guide the student toward the right way of living, the student may later appreciate their concern and attention.

第五，用服務結緣：

　幫你寫字，幫你掃地，幫你洗衣服，幫你服務，在自己也許只是舉手之勞，卻和對方結了緣。

5. Form connections through service

Helping someone to write, clean the floor, wash clothes, or helping them by performing some other type of task is forming good connections through service. Such service may be as effortless as lifting a finger, yet it may be sufficient to form good connections with others.

第六，用身體結緣：

　比方說我和對方合掌、微笑、點頭，甚至勞動、工作，這都是身體結緣。

6. Form connections through the physical body

Gestures such as a warm smile, an acknowledgement, or respectfully joining the palms can help to form connections with others. Physical labor is also a way to form these bonds.

所以，世間上最寶貴的就是廣結善緣，我們應該經常：

第一，用經濟結緣。

第二，用語言結緣。

第三，用功德結緣。

第四，用教育結緣。

Therefore, the most precious act in life is to broaden good connections. We should always:

1. Form connections through economy.
2. Form connections through speech.
3. Form connections through merits.
4. Form connections through education.

第五，用服務結緣。

第六，用身體結緣。

5. Form connections through service.

6. Form connections through the physical body.

如何廣結善緣 （二）

人與人之間，是靠著緣份在維持關係。所以人際關係其實就是因緣法。如何廣結善緣？我還有五點意見：

第一，用時間結緣：

有時候我們撥出一小時、二小時，聽聽別人抒解心裡的煩憂，給他一些安慰、鼓勵，這也是結緣。每個人一天有二十四小時，一年有三百六十五天，一生有幾十歲月。時間這麼多，花一些時間跟人結緣又有何妨？

第二，用空間結緣：

我把椅子讓給你坐，把房子借

How to Strengthen Our Affinity with Others (II)

Interpersonal relations are actually formed by good causal connections. Good causal connections maintain relationships between people. How does one form good connections? I have five suggestions:

1. Form temporal connections

Sometimes we can spend an hour or two listening to the worries of others. While listening to a person's problems, we can give him or her comfort and encouragement. This is an aspect of forming good connections. Everyone has twenty-four hours in a day, 365 days in a year, and hundreds of months in one's lifetime. With so much time, surely we can spend a little time forming connections with others.

2. Form spatial connections

When I let you sit in my chair and provide you with shelter, I am

給你住，這是空間結緣。過去有一個青年，為了跟鄰居爭一牆之地，千里迢迢寫信請在朝為官的父親幫忙，父親很明理，回了一封信說：「萬里投書只為牆，讓他三尺有何妨？長城萬里今猶在，不見當年秦始皇。」能夠留一點空間給人，就是結緣。有的人佔用建地，不給建大樓，幾年過去，就是不肯給人方便，這又何必呢？所謂地盡其利，我們應該把土地空間做最有價值的運用。

forming spatial connections. There was once a young man, who, after arguing with his neighbor over the boundary of a wall, wrote a letter to his father, an official who worked thousands of miles away. The father was very reasonable, replying in a letter saying, "Because of a wall, you sent me this letter from thousands of miles away. Would it hurt to give away three feet? Although the Great Wall of China still stands, the First Emperor of Qin Dynasty who built it has long since passed away." Giving others a little space is also a way of forming connections. Some people occupy many parcels of land, but they will not allow others to build on the land. They are simply unwilling to accommodate others. Is this necessary? As it is said, to maximize the benefits of the land, we need to make the most valuable use of space.

第三，用物資結緣：

每年冬天，佛光山舉辦冬令賑濟，以金錢、物品和貧苦人家結緣，這就是物資結緣，也是一種慈悲、歡喜的結緣。

3. Form connections with material goods

Every winter, the Fo Guang Shan Monastic Order sponsors a wintertime charity relief function to form connections with the poor. This is forming connections with material necessities, and it is also a means of forming connections of compassion and joyfulness.

第四，用技藝結緣：

技藝結緣是一種技能的傳授，譬如我會打字、打電腦、彈鋼琴，我把要領、訣竅傳授給你，這種技藝結緣也是一種助緣。

4. Form connections with skills

When we pass on the knowledge of our abilities to others, we are forming connections with skills. For example, I can type, operate a computer, and play a piano. I want to teach the main points of each skill to you. This kind of forming connections with skills is also a type of "helping" connection.

第五，用歡喜結緣：

世界上沒有比歡喜更寶貴的東西，有時我們用再多的金錢、物資送給別人，別人未必很歡喜。不如給人一個笑容，給人幾句讚美的話，用歡喜結緣，不但不需要付出辛苦代價，並且有很大的收穫。

5. Form connections of joyfulness

Nothing in the world is more precious than joyfulness. Sometimes, even if we give others a lot of money or material things, they do not necessarily feel very joyful. Instead, we should give warm smiles, words of praise, and happiness to others. Forming connections of joyfulness does not require much effort and can generate great happiness and huge rewards.

所以如何廣結善緣？就是：

第一，用時間結緣。
第二，用空間結緣。
第三，用物資結緣。
第四，用技藝結緣。
第五，用歡喜結緣。

There are five ways to broaden good connections:

1. Form temporal connections.
2. Form spatial connections.
3. Form connections with material goods.
4. Form connections with skills.
5. Form connections of joyfulness.

健康與長壽

Attaining Health and Longevity

所謂健康，一般人只想到身體的健康。雖然沒有頭痛，腸胃也沒毛病，但這還不算健康。如何求得健康與長壽。各有四個要訣：

健康上要注意：

When discussing the subject of health, we often tend to think only of physical health. But, just because a person is not presently experiencing a physical ailment, such as a headache or a stomach ache, it does not necessarily mean that he or she is healthy. How then can we strive for good health and longevity? There are four key points for attaining each goal.

For good health, please pay attention to the following:

第一，身體上的健康：
這當然是最必要的條件。

1. Health in our bodies
This, of course, is the most important requirement.

第二，心理上的健康：
我們的心，藏有貪欲、瞋恨、嫉妒、傲慢、邪見的毛病，等我們把心理的毛病都去除了，就能有心理的健康，如慈悲喜捨、戒定慧。

2. Health in our minds
Our minds harbor a variety of illnesses: desire, hatred, envy, arrogance, and perversion. When we rid ourselves of all illnesses of the mind, we attain mental health. Some approaches to attaining good mental health include practicing kindness, compassion, joy, equanimity, discipline, meditation, and wisdom.

第三，事業上的健康：

　要從事非法的事業。殺害生命、竊盜，甚至於算命卜卦，都是不如法的事業。要做正當的事業，才是健康的事業。

第四，信仰上的健康：

　不要邪信，以免遺憾終生。

　健康之後再求長壽。長壽，不僅是肉體活到八十歲、一百二十歲，就叫長壽，最要緊的，除了肉體上的長壽以外，我們還要有：

第一，言教上的長壽：

　意思指的是：我的一句話能流傳，我的教育能被大家接受，這就是我的長壽。

第二，工作上的長壽：

　工作要有恒，要敬慎持久。

3. Health in our careers

We must not engage in illegal business. Murder and burglary are unlawful; even fortune-telling and divining are not in accordance with Buddhist teachings. Our careers will be healthy only if we engage in lawful and just business practices.

4. Health in our beliefs

Do not believe in evil; it can ruin our lives. Evil will never make us healthy.

Once we have attained good health, we can seek to extend the meaning and impact of our lives. Thus, longevity refers not only to physically living for 80 or 120 years; it has broader meanings.

1. Longevity through education

When our words can be passed on to others, and people are thereby educated, we have achieved longevity.

2. Longevity through work

Longevity is accomplished when we are attentive and persistent in performing our work.

第三，功德上的長壽：

要有益於人類、社會，讓功德能持之以久。造一條路，可以讓眾人走幾百年；造一座橋，可以讓眾人走很久，就是功德上的長壽。

第四，法身上的長壽：

就是讓我們的精神不死，慧命永恆。人並非長生不死，能證悟不死的生命，才是一種無量壽的長壽。

吾人所求的健康如下：

第一，身體上的健康。
第二，心理上的健康。
第三，事業上的健康。
第四，信仰上的健康。

3. Longevity through virtue

We should benefit mankind and society and let the gifts of our virtues last for many years. When we help to pave a road, people can walk on it for hundreds of years. When we facilitate the construction of a bridge, people can use it for a long time. This is attaining longevity through virtue.

4. Longevity through the embodiment of the teachings

Embodying the teachings allows our spiritual life to live forever and the teachings to be permanent. After all, human beings have a limited life span. Only the spiritual life is limitless. This is the true longevity of life.

For good health we should maintain the following:

1. Health in our bodies.
2. Health in our minds.
3. Health in our careers.
4. Health in our beliefs.

吾人所求的長壽如下：

第一，言教上的長壽。
第二，工作上的長壽。
第三，功德上的長壽。
第四，法身上的長壽。

To have true longevity we should strive for the following:

1. Longevity through education.
2. Longevity through work.
3. Longevity through virtue.
4. Longevity through the embodiment of the teachings.

如何增廣福報

人人都希望自己的福德因緣深厚，因為有時候增加財富，財富不一定是我們的，增加物質、財富有時反而是個累贅。唯有福報是真的，到哪裏都享用不完。

如何增廣福報呢？

第一，少貪多捨：

捨就是一種布施、結緣，緣結得愈多，就像播了種，必有收成。所以少貪多捨，必能增廣福報。

第二，少聚多散：

不要積聚財富，因為財富是五家所共有。遇到水災、火災、貪官污吏、盜賊及不肖子孫，財富轉眼成空。錢要用了才是

How to Add to Our Blessings

Everyone wishes for an abundant store of blessings. After all, wealth is not permanent, and sometimes an excess of wealth and material prosperity can actually burden us with heavy responsibilities. In contrast, our store of blessings is always with us and is always a source of immense happiness.

How do we increase our blessings?

1. More giving, less grasping

Giving is a form of charity and it helps us form good causal relationships with others. Forming a multitude of good causal relationships with others is like planting numerous good seeds from which we will definitely reap a good harvest. If we can give instead of grasp, we can increase our blessings.

2. More sharing, less hoarding

If we want to increase our blessings, we should not be obsessed with accumulating wealth. Our wealth can disappear in five different ways: it can be lost in a

自己的，因此要多布施、多結緣。

flood, in a fire, to corrupt government officials, to thieves, or to prodigal offspring. Only if we use our wealth judiciously can our riches truly be ours.

Thus, we should use our wealth to give alms and to form good causal relationships with others.

第三，少執多放：

人不要太執著，執著於一點往往失去全部。要把眼光放大、放遠、放開，要能放得下，才能提得起。

3. More letting go, less clinging

We should not cling to our desires or expectations. By becoming too attached to a particular aspect of an issue, we will end up losing out on the whole thing. We should broaden, further, and free our perspectives. We have to learn to let go before we can pick up again.

第四，少傲多謙：

做人要謙虛，所謂「滿招損，謙受益」。太自滿、太傲慢，讓人看不起，謙虛的人才會受尊敬。

4. More humbleness, less pride

We all should learn to be humble. An old saying reminds us that "arrogance invites harm; humility begets benefits." People look down on those who are arrogant and conceited. Only a truly humble person can command respect.

第五，少私多公：

人不能只為自己而活，因此不

5. More altruism, less egoism

We must not forget that we are social beings; no one can survive

要處處只為自己著想。要常常想到別人,想到大眾,能夠少私多公,才能融入大眾,才能擴大小我。

without the help of other people. Thus, we should consider not only ourselves, but also the needs of others — of the common good. When we are concerned about the lives and well-being of others rather than merely our own needs and wants, we will be appreciated and accepted by others and our awareness of life will grow.

第六,少憂多喜:

人生苦短,不要讓生命充塞太多的憂鬱、傷感。要把歡樂、喜悅常駐心頭,並且影響他人。

6. More happiness, fewer worries

Life is short and full of suffering. We should not be preoccupied with our unhappy moments. We should think of the happy moments in our lives and let our joyful outlook influence others.

第七,少愛多慈:

愛是有污染性的、是自私的、是不究竟的。唯有把愛昇華為慈悲,才能平等對待一切眾生,才能對人有所助益,所以我們要少愛多慈。

7. More compassion, less mundane love

Mundane love is possessive and limited; it is far from perfect. When we transform mundane love into compassion and view all sentient beings through the eyes of equanimity, we can truly help others. Thus, we should develop more compassion and foster less mundane love.

第八，少色多德：

不要把生命浪費在愛情、美色的追求上。因為愛情、美色會隨著時間的遷流而產生變化。我們應該在道德、修養上用功，這才是永恆不滅的。

第九，少自多他：

不要凡事只想到自己，要想到自己以外還有別人。包括父母、兄弟、姊妹、兄弟、同學、朋友、同胞，及一切眾生。

第十，少拒多容：

泰山不辭土壤才能成其大。所以，能夠少拒多容，才會增加福報。

8. More virtues, less perishable beauty

We should not waste our time in the pursuit perishable beauty. Perishable beauty is impermanent and will change over the course of time. Only the cultivation of virtues and the enhancement of morality are everlasting.

9. More for others, less for ourselves

We should not just think about ourselves. We should also think about others, such as our parents, our brothers, our sisters, our friends, and all other sentient beings.

10. More acceptance, less discrimination

Tai Shan (a mountain in China) is big because it does not reject any type of soil. If we can be more accepting and less discriminating, we can increase our blessings.

如何增廣福報：

第一，少貪多捨。

第二，少聚多散。

第三，少執多放。

第四，少傲多謙。

第五，少私多公。

第六，少憂多喜。

第七，少愛多慈。

第八，少色多德。

第九，少自多他。

第十，少拒多容。

The ten ways to increase our blessings:

1. More giving, less grasping.
2. More sharing, less hoarding.
3. More letting go, less clinging.
4. More humbleness, less pride.
5. More altruism, less egoism.
6. More happiness, fewer worries.
7. More compassion, less mundane love.
8. More virtues, less perishable beauty.
9. More for others, less for ourselves.
10. More acceptance, less discrimination.

About the Author

Venerable Master Hsing Yun was born in Chiangdu, Chiangsu province, China, in 1927. Tonsured under Venerable Master Zhikai at age twelve, he became a novice monk at Mount Qixia Monastery and Jiaoshan College. He was fully ordained in 1941, and is the 48th Patriarch of the Linji (Rinzai) Chan School.

He went to Taiwan in 1949 where he undertook revitalizing Chinese Mahayana Buddhism on the Island with a range of activities novel for its time. He founded the Fo Guang Shan (Buddha's Light Mountain) Buddhist Order in 1967, and has established more than a hundred temples in Taiwan and on every continent since. In 1988, Hsi Lai Temple, the United States Headquarters was built outside Los Angeles.

At present, there are about twelve hundred nuns and two hundred monks in the Fo Guang Shan Order. The organization also includes sixteen Buddhist colleges, four publishing houses, four universities (one of which is the Hsi Lai University in California), a secondary school, a television station, an orphanage, and a home for the aged.

A prolific writer and an inspiring speaker, the Venerable Master has written many books on Buddhist sutras and a wide spectrum of topics over the past five decades. Most of his speeches and lectures were compiled into essays defining Humanistic Buddhism and outlining its practice. Some of his writings and sermons have been translated into different languages such as English, Spanish, German, Russian, Japanese, Korean, and Bengali. Examples of his writings available in English are *Hsing Yun Ch'an Talk (Peter Lang)*, *Being Good; Buddhist Ethics for Everyday Life (Weatherhill)*, and *Only A Great Rain; A Guide to Chinese Buddhist Meditation (Wisdom)*.

Venerable Master Hsing Yun is also the founder of Buddha's Light International Association, a worldwide organization of lay Buddhists dedicated to the propagation of Buddhism, with over 120 chapters and more than a million in membership.

About the Translator

As long as the time that Venerable Master Hsing Yun has been a Buddhist monk, he strongly believes that books and other documentations of the Buddha's teachings are the way to unite us all emotionally, to help us practice Buddhism at a higher altitude, and continuously define as well as challenge our views on living our lives.

In 1996, the Fo Guang Shan International Translation Center was established with this goal in mind. This marked the beginning of a string of publications translated into various languages from the Master's original writings in Chinese. Presently, several offices have been set up worldwide, namely in Los Angeles and San Diego, USA; Sydney, Australia; Berlin, Germany; Argentina; South Africa; Korea; and Japan; to coordinate translation or publication-related projects with each other.

The Fo Guang Shan International Translation Center is a non-profit agency. All proceeds from our book sales support Buddhist propagation efforts. We welcome any comments and suggestions that our readers may have regarding our publications.

Fo Guang Shan International Translation Center
3456 South Glenmark Drive
Hacienda Heights, CA 91745
U.S.A.
Tel: 626-923-5143   Fax: 626-923-5145
Email: itc@blia.org   Website: www.blia.org

Printed in the United States
2095